SOCIAL SECURITY

FROM **MEDICARE** TO **SPOUSAL** **101**
BENEFITS, AN ESSENTIAL PRIMER ON
GOVERNMENT RETIREMENT AID

ALFRED MILL

▲ **adams**media
Avon, Massachusetts

Published by
Adams Media, a division of F+W Media, Inc.
57 Littlefield Street, Avon, MA 02322. U.S.A.
www.adamsmedia.com

Contains material adapted from *The Everything® Retirement Planning Book* by
Judith B. Harrington and Stanley J. Steinberg, CFP, copyright © 2007 by F+W Media, Inc.,
ISBN 10: 1-59869-207-0, ISBN 13: 978-1-59869-207-5 and *The Everything® Personal Finance
in Your 20s & 30s Book, 3rd Edition* by Howard Davidoff, JD, CPA, LLM, copyright © 2012 by
F+W Media, Inc., ISBN 10: 1-4405-4256-2, ISBN 13: 978-1-4405-4256-5.

ISBN 10: 1-4405-9922-X
ISBN 13: 978-1-4405-9922-4
eISBN 10: 1-4405-9923-8
eISBN 13: 978-1-4405-9923-1

Printed in the United States of America.

10   9   8   7   6   5   4   3   2   1

Cover design by Heather McKiel.
Cover images © Clipart.com.
Interior images © iStockphoto.com/zimmytws/larryhw/Laura Young/MariuszBlach;
Global Cuts; 123RF/Robert Mizerek/zimmytws/Brian Jackson/racorn/iqoncent/dmbaker.

This book is available at quantity discounts for bulk purchases.
For information, please call 1-800-289-0963.

CONTENTS

INTRODUCTION 5

WHAT IS SOCIAL SECURITY?. 7

THE BEGINNINGS OF SOCIAL SECURITY. 12

THE HISTORY OF RETIREMENT. 18

THE RISE OF AMERICA'S MIDDLE CLASS. 20

FUNDING SOCIAL SECURITY 24

FIXING SOCIAL SECURITY 28

GETTING A SOCIAL SECURITY CARD 34

PROTECTING YOUR SOCIAL SECURITY NUMBER 42

QUALIFICATIONS FOR RECEIVING BENEFITS 47

YOUR FULL RETIREMENT AGE 52

GETTING STARTED WITH SOCIAL SECURITY 55

ESTIMATING YOUR BENEFITS. 60

DISABILITY BENEFITS 65

SUPPLEMENTAL SECURITY INCOME. 72

CHILDREN WITH DISABILITIES 77

SPOUSAL BENEFITS. 82

SURVIVORS BENEFITS 87

OTHER BENEFICIARIES 92

BENEFITS FOR CHILDREN 97

TAXES ON SOCIAL SECURITY BENEFITS 102

WORKING IN RETIREMENT. 106

TAKING BENEFITS EARLY. 111

CLAIMING BENEFITS LATER. 117

IF YOU'RE SELF-EMPLOYED. 122

DEEMED FILING 126

WINDFALL ELIMINATION PROVISION 131

GOVERNMENT PENSION OFFSET 137

THE RETROACTIVE LUMP-SUM OPTION 140

STOPPING YOUR BENEFITS 144

APPEALING AN SSA DECISION 148

HEALTH AND SOCIAL SECURITY 153

MEDICARE 159

EXTRA HELP WITH PRESCRIPTION COSTS 167

MEDICARE ADVANTAGE 172

MEDICAID 178

SOCIAL SECURITY AND YOUR RETIREMENT 184

USING A FINANCIAL PLANNER 192

PLANNING FOR TOMORROW 197

FINDING HAPPINESS IN RETIREMENT 213

YOUR DREAM RETIREMENT 217

IF A DOOR CLOSES 219

THE NEW RETIREMENT 224

INDEX 235

INTRODUCTION

When you think about your retirement, whether it's coming up soon or many years away, you'll start to think about Social Security. Since the Social Security program is going to be an essential part of your golden years, and since you've probably heard people say that it's running out of money, you'll probably have a lot of questions:

How much money will I get?

How does the government calculate that figure?

Will my Social Security benefits be taxed? If so, how much?

Is the program going broke? Will there even be any money by the time I retire?

A whopping 74 percent of single people and 52 percent of married couples are going to depend on Social Security payments for more than half their income in retirement. But for something so financially important, many people know very little about Social Security.

Social Security 101 will give you the most up-to-date information about this government program. You'll learn how to apply for benefits and when you should start taking them. You'll also learn strategies to maximize the benefits you receive and about recent changes to Social Security laws, changes that affect your filing plans.

Like any part of the government, the Social Security Administration can seem intimidating. *Social Security 101* will explain to you how this agency works and how you can appeal its decision about your benefits if you don't agree with it. You'll also learn about the government healthcare programs Medicare and Medicaid and how they relate to your Social Security benefits.

Social Security is an important component of a carefully thought-out retirement plan. It is in your best interest to learn as much as you can about how Social Security works so that you can be sure to receive all the money that's coming to you. This book will be an essential part of the toolkit you can use to build a financially secure retirement.

WHAT IS SOCIAL SECURITY?

A Retirement Plan for Everyone

On the first day of your first full-time job, retirement was probably the last thing on your mind. You were too busy wondering how to learn all your duties, impress your boss, and find out where the bathrooms and the coffee machine were located. You were thinking about this amazing new world of work you'd just stepped into and what kind of people you were going to meet and work with. All in all, it was probably one of the most exciting days of your life. Retirement—if it even crossed your mind—was something far off in the misty future. Chances are, the subject of Social Security was something that didn't even remotely intrude into your consciousness.

Although you may not have been thinking about Social Security, the Social Security Administration (SSA) was already thinking about you.

With your first paycheck, you took a step into the complex government program called Social Security. For the rest of your working career, that program tracks you. And when you finally decide to retire at the age of sixty-two or older, you'll apply to the SSA for the benefits you've accumulated in the course of your working life.

As you begin to approach your full retirement age (more about that later), you'll probably give more and more thought to Social Security:

- How much are my benefits per month going to amount to?
- What if it's not enough for me to live on?
- I keep hearing that Social Security is going bankrupt. What if all the money's gone by the time I retire?
- Where can I go for help in figuring this stuff out?

These are all good questions, and there are certainly plenty of others. Social Security has been around for a long time, and it's seen its fair share of changes and adjustments. This has led to a seemingly byzantine set of rules and regulations. We'll explain the most important of these as we go on, but for right now the important thing is for you to understand clearly what Social Security is.

SOCIAL INSURANCE

At its most basic, Social Security is a form of social insurance, set up and administered by the U.S. government. Payments to you from the system can begin as early as age sixty-two (although there are good reasons not to take your benefits that early, as we'll see) and will continue until you die. It's essentially a government-run retirement program that aims to keep you and your fellow retirees out of poverty.

The program is funded through taxes, which are collected directly from workers' paychecks. Look on your latest paycheck stub and find the acronym FICA. The amount next to it is how much money from your paycheck went toward Social Security.

FICA and SECA

FICA stands for Federal Insurance Contributions Act. The Social Security tax is also sometimes designated SECA, which stands for Self-Employment Contributions Act. This latter tax is levied on people who are self-employed (as the name implies). Some portion of both taxes also goes toward the governmental medical program, Medicare.

Payouts from the Social Security program are huge; according to the Social Security Administration, in 2015 about 59 million people in the United States received Social Security benefits. Total payouts through the program amounted to almost $870 billion in 2015. The number of people receiving Social Security benefits is expected to rise as members of the baby boom generation retire, something that has created concerns that the program might go bankrupt.

Some Facts and Figures

Here are some things you may not know about Social Security:

- Nine out of ten people aged sixty-five and older receive Social Security benefits.
- Social Security covers an estimated 165 million workers (in the sense that anyone who pays payroll taxes to Social Security is "covered").
- Of those receiving benefits, 39.5 million get retirement benefits; 6.1 million receive survivors benefits; and 9 million receive disability benefits.
- About one in four of today's twenty-year-olds will become disabled before reaching age sixty-seven.
- In today's workforce, 51 percent of workers do not have private pension coverage.

We'll consider this question later and look at some possible ways in which Social Security might be fixed, but for right now we'll look at the program as it currently exists.

The taxes collected through workers' paychecks go into one of a series of trust funds: The Federal Old-Age and Survivors Insurance Trust Fund, the Federal Disability Insurance Trust Fund, the Federal Hospital Insurance Trust Fund, and the Federal Supplemental

Medical Insurance Trust Fund. Your earnings are taxed for these funds up to a certain federally determined limit. As of 2015, the maximum amount of taxable income was $118,500. Any money you make beyond that cap isn't taxed for Social Security (although, of course, it is taxed in other ways such as income tax).

The Social Security Administration also operates other important programs, including the State Children's Health Insurance Program (SCHIP) and Supplemental Security Income (SSI). The SSA, which has its headquarters in Maryland, has ten regional offices scattered around the United States and employs more than 67,000 people.

The agency issues a nine-digit number to all U.S. citizens and temporary working residents. This number is used to track people within the Social Security system, but it has also become an important identification number that is used in many circumstances to guarantee personal security (for instance, in banking transactions).

Baby Names Lists

As a by-product of issuing Social Security numbers to newborns, the SSA is very up on the popularity of baby names for any given year since the system started. Every year the SSA issues two lists: one for the ten most popular girls' names and another for the ten most popular boys' names. Go to www.ssa.gov/OACT/babynames to check out the most recent lists.

The way in which Social Security has been administered has changed over the years, reflecting changing economic circumstances within the country. The most recent change came in 2015, when Congress passed a law that eliminated several filing strategies (particularly the strategy called file and suspend) that had been gaining in popularity.

In general, Social Security mostly benefits lower-paid workers, since these are the people who are unlikely to be able to save enough for retirement on their own. However, anyone who pays into the system by working as an employee or who is self-employed and pays Social Security taxes can become eligible to receive benefits. This is a controversial aspect of the program, and some have suggested there should be an upper income level beyond which people wouldn't receive benefits (since, presumably, they could afford to support themselves in retirement without aid from the government). Warren Buffett, one of the richest people in the United States, has pointed out the absurdity of the fact that he receives Social Security benefits.

You're also eligible for benefits if you've just been released from prison. You can't receive benefits while you're in jail (provided you've been incarcerated for thirty continuous days), but once you're released, you can begin or restart your benefits.

In addition to paying out retirement checks, the Social Security Trust Funds also make payments to people who are disabled to the degree that they are unable to work. In 2013, this part of the funds made payments of around $140 billion. Another part of the program, the Supplemental Security Income (SSI), pays money to low-income people who are sixty-five or older, blind, or disabled. Some would argue that this isn't really part of the Social Security system, since it's funded from the general funds of U.S. Treasury rather than the Social Security Trust Funds. But it's still administered by the SSA.

THE BEGINNINGS OF SOCIAL SECURITY

Roots in the Great Depression

In the late 1920s Americans were convinced that they had life by the tail. It was the jazz age, the Roaring Twenties—"flappers" in fringed skirts and bobbed hair frolicked in nightclubs, accompanied by scores of eager young men. Bootlegged champagne flowed freely, and dancers puffed on cigarettes while downing that new American innovation, cocktails. Inventions such as the telephone, moving pictures, and above all, the automobile spread across the country, changing both the physical and cultural face of the United States. Above all, there was prosperity. World War I, which had devastated Europe and destroyed a generation of young men, had barely touched America. Far from the death and destruction of Europe, American factories turned out hundreds of millions of dollars in commodities that poured into eager markets.

The stock market was intoxicated by this wealth. Stock prices soared to higher and higher levels. Analysts predicted an endless bull market; prices would continue to go up and up.

Alas, it was not to be! Beginning on October 24, 1929, the American stock market precipitously crashed. Over a two-day period, the Dow Jones Industrial Average fell 23 percent. The demand for manufactured goods dried up, seemingly overnight. Businesses collapsed, industries shrank, and millions were thrown out of work. President Herbert Hoover's responses to the economic chaos were neither swift nor imaginative enough to stem the tide. Across the country, homeless workers erected shantytowns, derisively named

Hoovervilles. Whatever small nest eggs had been accumulated by workers for their old age were wiped out overnight. Popular anger with Hoover and the Republican Party helped sweep Franklin D. Roosevelt into the presidency in 1933.

A less likely champion of the common man and woman could scarcely be imagined. Roosevelt came from an aristocratic clan that numbered President Theodore Roosevelt as among its most distinguished member. Franklin's mother, Sara, came from a New York family whose fortune was founded on the opium trade with China. The young Franklin attended Groton School, a private school in Groton, Massachusetts, and then went on to Harvard. At some stage, he learned to sympathize with the plight of those less fortunate than himself. This compassion for the poor and needy colored much of his political career.

Upon assuming the presidency, Roosevelt developed and expanded many programs begun by Hoover, and he also launched a series of new initiatives. Collectively, he dubbed this effort the New Deal. The New Deal was composed of two parts: The first part, the First New Deal, from 1933–34, is sometimes referred to as "The First Hundred Days," since the laws that created the new programs were passed during the first 100 days of Roosevelt's administration. In this First New Deal period the president's actions focused on unemployment and the need for immediate relief of poverty-stricken workers. During the so-called Second New Deal, which lasted from 1935–36, Roosevelt was able to contemplate the economy and the country in a broader, more leisured perspective.

With the issues of poverty and joblessness much on his mind, Roosevelt was disturbed to see that Dr. Francis Townsend had proposed a plan for the government to take care of people in their old age. Townsend proposed the government pay everyone over sixty years old a monthly sum of $200. His only restriction was that they not have a criminal past.

Townsend's proposal was extremely popular—so much so that Roosevelt was concerned lest he not have a viable alternative before the 1936 presidential election. Under these circumstances, he asked Secretary of Labor Frances Perkins to come up with a plan to counter Townsend's.

Frances Perkins

Frances Perkins (1880–1965) was the first woman to serve in the U.S. Cabinet. She held the post of Secretary of Labor from 1933 to 1945, the longest-serving secretary in that position.

Perkins and the committee that assisted her studied the issue from many different angles and eventually produced a report. The report, in turn, spurred the writing and passage of a bill in 1935: the Social Security Act.

Bismarck and the German Precedent

One of the important precedents studied by Perkins's committee was the social insurance created under Prussian Chancellor Otto von Bismarck in the previous century. Though a die-hard conservative, Bismarck in 1889 set up a system of old-age insurance that required payments from both workers and employers. His goal was to prevent the implementation of some more radical scheme. When accused of socialism on account of his program, Bismarck could point to his long political record of hostility to socialism and communism.

THE SCOPE OF THE ACT

The 1935 law passed by Congress was limited in scope compared to what Social Security covers today. The preamble says the act is:

> An act to provide for the general welfare by establishing a system of Federal old-age benefits, and by enabling the several States to make more adequate provision for aged persons, blind persons, dependent and crippled children, maternal and child welfare, public health, and the administration of their unemployment compensation laws; to establish a Social Security Board; to raise revenue; and for other purposes.

The act excluded almost half of U.S. workers from Social Security coverage; only gradually did it expand to cover most of the population.

John G. Winant

President Roosevelt asked John G. Winant to become the first head of the Social Security Board, charged with carrying out the provisions of the 1935 act. Winant was a former three-term governor of New Hampshire and a member of the Republican Party. After the party's vice presidential candidate in the 1936 elections, Alf Landon, began campaigning against Social Security, Winant resigned from the board in order to defend Social Security against Landon's attacks.

The Social Security Administration, which grew out of the Social Security Board, was at first an independent agency. It became part of a sub-Cabinet department, the Federal Security Agency, in 1939, and then, in 1995, resumed its status as an independent agency of the Federal government.

THE FIRST BENEFICIARIES

When the program formally began in 1937, employers and workers paid 1 percent tax each on the worker's income up to $3,000. Benefits began to be paid out in 1940 (they were originally scheduled for 1942 but were moved up by a 1939 amendment to the act). In that year, Ernest Ackerman of Cleveland became the first person to receive a Social Security benefit—all of seventeen cents. His pay had been taxed five cents.

The first monthly payment went to Ida May Fuller of Vermont. Between 1937 and 1939 she paid in $24.75 to the system. Starting in January 1940 she received monthly benefits of $22.54. Since she lived to be 100 years old, her benefits at the end of her life totaled $22,888.92. She commented, "It wasn't that I expected anything, mind you, but I knew I'd been paying for something called Social Security."

"We can never insure 100 percent of the population against 100 percent of the hazards and vicissitudes of life, but we have tried to frame a law which will give some measure of protection to the average citizen and to his family against the loss of a job and against poverty-ridden old age."

—President Franklin D. Roosevelt

Expanding Beneficiaries

In 1950, Congress expanded the range of people covered to include some agricultural workers, domestic workers, nonprofit employees, and those self-employed. By 1954, that range had grown to include all agricultural labor, hotel and laundry workers, and employees of state and local government. In the 1960s, the number of people covered continued to increase, including disabled adult children of workers covered under the act. Today, as previously mentioned, an estimated 165 million workers are covered by Social Security—an impressive feat for a program more than eighty years old.

THE HISTORY OF RETIREMENT

The Evolution of Leisure

Earlier we talked about the history of Social Security and how it grew out of the Great Depression and the New Deal policies of Franklin Roosevelt's administration. It's time to put this in a broader context, to consider how the concept of life after work developed. It is a pretty recent phenomenon that itself is closely linked to the move from an agrarian to an industrial society, paired with the tremendous strides in healthcare over the past century and a half.

As mentioned earlier, many people credit Otto von Bismarck, as chancellor of Germany in the late nineteenth century, with laying the groundwork for Social Security. In fact, Bismarck should be credited with developing the concept of retirement itself by establishing a pension for military personnel. He was no fool, recklessly frittering away government funds. He set the age at which a soldier could begin collecting his pension at sixty-five. That would be like setting the retirement age for today at 125 because, in that era, the average life expectancy for Germans was the mid-thirties. The actuarial number-crunchers of that era would have had no problem with a pension as a concept under this age restriction because, statistically, who would live to collect?

Don't think the bean counters in the United States had a much bigger heart when Social Security legislation was first passed in 1935. At the beginning of this hallmark entitlement program for Americans, the age for receiving benefits was set at sixty-five, which sounds great, even normal by today's standards. But what you might not know is that American life expectancy at that time was only sixty-two, meaning that the government had limited financial exposure with this sweeping program. Further, as the legislation was originally written only about 60 percent of the working population, those in commerce and industry, qualified for Social Security. In fact, the first checks did not begin to flow until 1940.

Expanding the Aging Population

Thanks to tremendous decreases in infant and child mortality through the first half of the twentieth century, the number of people alive today that are at least sixty-five years old is equal to half of all the people who have ever lived to age sixty-five in the course of written history.

In the 1950s, benefits were added to Social Security and the overall umbrella expanded to cover government employees, farmers, domestic help, and the self-employed. An added feature to the legislation was that workers could begin receiving reduced benefits at age sixty-two if they chose. Women became eligible for benefits in their own right in 1961. In 1965 hospital benefits were added, which became the basis for the Medicare and Medicaid coverage that today's seniors are fighting tooth and nail to protect. Social Security marched right along through the early 1970s, adding built-in cost-of-living adjustments (COLA). It wasn't until the late 1970s that the brakes started to be applied. During the decades following World War II, while Social Security was ramping up, private pension plans designed to mesh with government programs were expanding. Even with the private pensions, however, it was Social Security that provided the financial bedrock for aging Americans.

There may not have been enough money through these programs to provide retirees with the dolce vita, but it was enough that, for the first time, legions of older workers could leave their jobs on their terms, not when they were ready to practically fall into an early grave.

THE RISE OF AMERICA'S MIDDLE CLASS

A Retired Class Is Born

Up to now we've largely talked about Social Security in terms of how it will affect you. But it's time to consider the wider impact of the program. In truth, Social Security was vital in creating what we've come to accept as a fact of life: the American middle class.

It's a bit startling to think that until the mid-twentieth century, the middle class didn't really exist, at least in the sense of a mass phenomenon. This went hand in hand with the fact that a retired class of people who stood out from the rest of the population didn't really exist either. That began to change, though, due in part to the vision of people like Del Webb.

A true American original, Webb was the real-estate developer who took a radical gamble with the creation of Sun City in Arizona. This was the landmark retirement community based on age segregation—no youngsters need apply—that became a model with three key characteristics:

- Activity—there would be plenty to do.
- Economy—houses would be affordable; costs for common facilities would be spread among all residents.
- Individuality—residents would be free to choose whatever they wanted to do.

The convergence of social policies after World War II helped make life at a Sun City type of retirement community possible.

Postwar, cheap government loans enabled young families to purchase their homes in mass numbers. These homes appreciated in value, creating an asset that could be cashed in when the go-to-work and the raise-the-kids jobs had been wrapped up. The expanding Social Security program laid the groundwork for predictable income in addition to the tangible asset that home ownership provided.

Social Security in Sweden

Not surprisingly, Sweden, often pointed to as an example of democratic socialism, has a firmly embedded system of government assistance for the elderly. Sweden's old-age pension begins at age sixty-one. Employers' contributions amount to 31.42 percent of the employee's gross salary. In many instances, state assistance is accompanied by private pensions. If you have a low income (or none) and have lived in Sweden for at least three years, you are entitled to an additional pension. With its extensive provisions for childcare, maternity leave, disability payments, and housing allowances, Sweden provides "cradle to grave" social insurance for its citizens.

At the same time, a shift was occurring in the family structure. In a preindustrial agrarian culture, every person was needed to work the land for as long as humanly possible. Older family members were valued for their knowledge. The family farm was needed for survival, and transferring ownership did not happen until the owner died. The younger family members cared for the aging or ill older members. This family ecosystem changed forever when new industries arose, and people became more mobile and were no longer tied to the land for survival.

Leisure Time

With people living longer, and having the financial flexibility to quit working, the question arose: "What to do?" In the mid-twentieth century, the thinking was to view retirement as a period of leisure. If work was a hard slog, then retirement would be the payoff with nothing to think about other than how to enjoy oneself. The notion of age-segregated communities ignited a positive response because now there would be a place for the oldsters to go who were no longer needed by their employers or their families. These communities were seen as a reward for a lifetime of hard work. One thing was clear: There was a very clean line between work and retirement. Work was work, and retirement was fun.

Social Security in Canada

Canadians aged sixty-five or older and who have an income less than $114,815 per year receive payments from the Old Age Security pension (OAS). If they make more than $71,592 per year, when tax time comes the OAS claws back some of that money at a rate of 15 percent of net income. You are eligible for the OAS scheme if you:

- Have lived in Canada for at least forty years from the time you turned eighteen
- Were born prior to July 1, 1952, and lived in Canada for at least ten years after turning eighteen; Canada has a reciprocal agreement with the United States that allows Canadian citizens who have lived in the United States for some time to count those years toward their qualifying time for the OAS

The Search for Something More Than Fun

Frenetic activity in the pursuit of fun hardly seems to define relaxation. The concept of luring a massive portion of the nation's population to reservations of recreation was an artificial design. Although keeping busy has its merits, it has its limits.

Not all seniors were decamping to retirement communities. Some, whether for lack of sufficient financial resources or simply lack of interest, were leaving work and going nowhere. All that experience, talent, and skill were sitting idle, waiting to be released in a meaningful direction. It should come as no surprise that today there is an explosion of new opportunities. People you know, and many you do not, are blazing paths and opening minds to a new understanding of what a happy retirement means.

FUNDING SOCIAL SECURITY

Paying It Forward

One of the most common myths about Social Security is that in some way it's a Ponzi scheme. This myth persists because the money you pay into the system isn't held in trust for when you retire but instead is used to pay benefits for workers who are retired *right now*.

What's a Ponzi Scheme?

This type of fraud, named after Charles Ponzi, who constructed such a scheme in 1920, pays old investors by using capital paid into the scheme by new investors. Since the scheme lures in investors by promising higher-than-average returns, it needs to continually expand in scope. The most famous Ponzi scheme was that of Bernard Madoff, who bilked investors out of $65 billion, the largest such fraud in history.

INVESTING ITS FUNDS

One of the most important things that differentiates Social Security from a Ponzi scheme is that the money in the Social Security Trust Funds is invested. An operator of a Ponzi scheme doesn't invest, since that wouldn't allow the scheme to pay out the high returns demanded by its investors. Social Security, on the other hand, invests in U.S. Treasury bonds, one of the safest investments in the world, since those bonds are backed by the full faith and credit of the United States.

Another important distinction is that Social Security is mandatory for U.S. workers. There's no possibility of people suddenly deciding to opt out of it. Most Ponzi schemes collapse when a portion of their investors decide to take their money out of what proves to be phantom investments. But that can't happen with Social Security.

RUNNING OUT OF MONEY?

Why, then, are there persistent rumors (louder during an election cycle) that Social Security is running out of money?

It's true that over the years the government has had to make adjustments to ensure that the system continues to have the wherewithal to pay benefits. When Social Security began in 1935, it taxed just 2 percent of a worker's earnings—1 percent came from the worker's paycheck and 1 percent was paid by her or his employer. It taxed up to $3,000 in income. Today that tax has risen to 12.4 percent of a worker's earnings, which is still split evenly between worker and employer, and the income level cap has been increased to $118,500. (Self-employed people pay a tax of 12.4 percent on their earnings.) So over time, Social Security taxes have increased.

Does the Government Raid Social Security?

Some people have charged that Social Security's difficulties, real or imagined, are caused by the government burrowing into its trust funds and spending the money on various other projects. In fact, this charge misunderstands the fact that these aren't really trust funds. They're government accounts, and the money from them is invested.

The government funds Social Security in three ways:

1. From payroll taxes collected on workers' paychecks. This is the FICA tax.
2. From money deposited in the Social Security Trust Funds, which is invested in Treasury bonds and earns interest. This money represents a surplus collected when taxed income exceeds the amount paid out in benefits.
3. From income tax that beneficiaries with high incomes pay on Social Security benefits.

Overall, the program is expected to run a surplus until 2020. However, the trust funds will be depleted sometime in the 2030s (exact dates vary, depending on who's doing the estimating). Even in that case, using payroll taxes and income tax, the program can continue to pay out 77 percent of benefits. However, as you'll see in the next chapter, there are a number of ways in which Social Security can be fixed that will make it solvent for a long time to come.

In addition to payroll taxes to fund Social Security, you and your employer each pay 1.45 percent tax to fund Medicare's Hospital Insurance Trust Fund. High-income individuals pay an additional 0.9 percent to support Medicare.

IS SOCIAL SECURITY UNFAIR TO YOUNG PEOPLE?

One argument that's been brought up a great deal is that Social Security is a burden on the younger generation. When the system was created, the argument goes, there were fifty-five workers to support each retiree, so the payroll tax each worker paid could be kept very low. But since 1935, the life expectancy of the average worker has dramatically increased. The result is that it takes more and more younger workers to support retired older ones. It's been estimated that to continue to function, the system needs approximately 2.8 younger workers for each retiree Social Security supports.

If the ratio slips below the critical level, we will reach a situation in which too few workers must support too many retirees. This is the crisis that doomsayers are warning about. But is the situation as dire as they claim? Let's look at what's really wrong with Social Security and how it can be fixed.

FIXING SOCIAL SECURITY

Countering the Myth of Collapse

Spend any time on the Internet and you'll come across someone claiming that Social Security is on the verge of collapse. Those people assert that the system is overwhelmed. Millions upon millions of newly retired baby boomers are filing claims every day. It's only a matter of time before the system runs out of money. The more extreme version of this assertion is that Social Security is a Ponzi scheme (we took up this point in the previous chapter) and as such has always been unstable and is fated to fail.

What's true and what's false about these claims?

WILL SOCIAL SECURITY GO BANKRUPT?

From 1985 to 2009, the government took in more money in payroll taxes for Social Security than it paid out in benefits. The resulting surplus went into the Social Security Trust Funds, where it earned interest. However, beginning in 2010, benefits exceeded revenues from payroll taxes. The result is that if this trend continues, the trust funds will run out of money around 2037. (Note that this assumes the economy grows at an average rate of 1.7 percent. A faster average growth would mean the system would remain fully solvent for much longer.)

All right. That looks pretty straightforward. That means the system will be bankrupt by 2037, right?

Well, no. It doesn't.

The reason is because Social Security is set up so that today's workers are paying the cost of today's retirees. In other words, there is *always* money coming into the system, because the American workforce continues to, well, work, and payroll taxes continue to be deducted from their paychecks. In addition, the system continues to have a revenue stream from wealthy individuals paying income tax on their benefits. The third revenue source, remember, is the interest earned by the surplus that went into the trusts. So the system can't go bankrupt in the sense of just running out of money.

Reduced Benefits

It is true that unless steps are taken by the government, by 2037 Social Security will no longer have the funds to pay full benefits to retirees unless the economy experiences a faster growth rate. At that point, experts estimate that tax revenues would only account for about 75–78 percent of full benefits.

Changes in the Past

Change is nothing new to Social Security. Over the years it has seen a number of adjustments, from the amount of payroll taxes deducted to cost-of-living adjustments (COLA). The tax rate first increased in 1950 from 2 percent to 3 percent. The following year, the upper limit on taxable income was raised for the first time from $3,000 to $3,600.

Although this is a long way from being bankrupt, it's something no one wants to see happen (especially anyone planning to retire in 2037 or later). Seventy-six million baby boomers started to become eligible for Social Security as of 2008 (that is, they began turning sixty-two). If the system is going to be able to handle those numbers, the politicians in Washington need to start considering some possible fixes.

HOW COULD SOCIAL SECURITY BE FIXED?

A number of possible changes to the system have been proposed to extend its solvency and ability to pay full benefits. Some of these are more politically possible than others, and almost all are controversial.

Privatize the System

At the beginning of his second term, President George W. Bush proposed the partial privatization of Social Security. His proposal would have allowed participants in the program to move some of their money to personalized investment accounts. The plan was aimed primarily at younger workers; older workers were exempt from it.

Although the plan had the backing of many conservatives, others opposed it, along with virtually all Democratic Party politicians. Bush campaigned energetically for the plan, but ultimately it failed to gain traction.

Many commentators pointed out that after the Great Recession of 2008–09 privatized accounts could have severely impacted many workers' retirement savings. It seems unlikely in the near future that any politician will be able to privatize Social Security, in part or in whole.

Raise the Earnings Cap or Payroll Tax

Under the present system, payroll taxes for Social Security are not deducted from earnings above $118,000. (As previously mentioned, this cap has been raised a number of times in the program's history; it started out at $3,000.) One relatively simple way to make the program solvent in the future is to raise this cap again. Taking it up to $229,500 would, it's estimated, cut the program's shortfall by 28 percent.

Another way to increase the amount of money in the system is to hike the payroll tax, which accounts for the large majority of revenue that flows into the system. Remember that this tax began in 1935 at 1 percent each from both worker and employer and is currently at 6.2 percent for each of them. It's estimated that if the tax were raised by 1 percent, to 7.2 percent for worker and employer, this alone could account for 50 percent of the program's shortfall.

That said, raising taxes is never easy, and it's hard to say whether Congress would have the political fortitude to take either of the steps just mentioned. In addition, since lower-earning workers get more of a return on their contributions than higher-earning workers, raising the earnings cap would be unpopular with richer contributors.

Expanding Coverage

Although Social Security covers the overwhelming majority of U.S. workers, some are still outside it. Roughly 25 percent of state and government workers use a pension system for their retirements rather than paying into Social Security. If the system were expanded to cover them as well, it's estimated that this could reduce the program's shortfall by about 6 percent. However, this would mean higher government contributions to pensions to fully compensate those workers who remain covered by them. For this reason, state and city governments generally oppose such a move.

Cut Benefits

The solutions proposed so far assume that the goal is for the system to continue to pay the same level of benefits. But suppose, instead, the government were to cut benefits. This would certainly help the program remain solvent. But who can imagine beneficiaries cheering about it? Such a program would have to be carefully phased in, would have to be graded from lower-earning workers to higher earners, and politically would be immensely unpopular.

Adjust the COLA

As mentioned earlier, the first cost-of-living adjustment in Social Security benefits was made in 1950. In 1975 Congress mandated automatic adjustments within the system. Benefits are currently tied to the Consumer Price Index for Urban Wage Earners and Clerical Workers (CPI-W). Some people have proposed changing this, and instead link benefits to what is called a chained Consumer Price Index (CPI). The details of this don't need to concern us here; suffice it to say that because the chained CPI rises a bit slower than the CPI-W, making this switch would save significant amounts of money in the long run—it would cut the shortfall by about 20 percent.

The downside to this, of course, is that beneficiaries would receive a lower cost of living increase, something that no one would welcome.

Raising the Full Retirement Age (FRA)

Finally, there's the option of increasing the age at which workers can take their full benefits. We'll talk later about how your FRA is calculated, but here we'll just note that in the current system, if you were born in 1960 or later you reach your FRA at age sixty-seven. (You can take benefits before then, but they'll be less than they would be if you waited until your FRA; more discussion of this later.) The argument has been made that since longevity is increasing, people should expect to work longer and therefore the FRA should be pushed back. Moving the FRA back a single year, to sixty-eight, could reduce the shortfall by up to 16 percent.

Of course, many people aren't enthusiastic about adding another year of work onto their careers. They want to get as many golden years as possible.

ESTIMATING THE POLITICAL PRICE

All of the solutions mentioned in this chapter have political costs, and none will, by itself, eliminate Social Security's shortfall. But it's likely that eventually some combination of these changes will be used to keep the program solvent at least into the next century.

GETTING A SOCIAL SECURITY CARD

Joining the System

When you start your first job, you must have a Social Security number (SSN); you can't be legally hired without it. So even though you technically aren't required to have a Social Security number, for all practical purposes you'll need one at some point in your life. As has been pointed out, Social Security numbers have become a basic means of identification for most Americans, precisely because they're so widespread.

HOW EARLY SHOULD YOU GET A CARD?

Many parents take care of the issue of Social Security numbers very early—pretty much when their baby is born. It's easiest to do this when you're giving information to the hospital, which they'll use to generate your child's birth certificate. The Social Security Administration points out that waiting longer can create delays while the SSA verifies the birth certificate.

To apply at a Social Security office, you'll need to bring proof of your baby's age, U.S. citizenship, and identity as well as proof of your own identity. Then you'll fill out Form SS-5. The SSA will take up to twelve weeks to issue your child a Social Security card. If your child is twelve or older, she or he must be present in person at the SSA office when you fill out the application.

Why on Earth Does a Baby Need a Social Security Number?

Good question. After all, the baby isn't going to get a job any time soon. But there are other reasons for her or him to have a Social Security number:

- If you're planning to claim your child as a dependent
- If you want to open a bank account in your baby's name
- If you're going to buy savings bonds for the child
- If you're getting medical coverage for your offspring
- If you're applying for government services for the child

The SSA only accepts certain documents as proof of citizenship. These include:

- U.S. birth certificate
- U.S. Consular Report of Birth Abroad
- U.S. passport
- Certificate of Naturalization
- Certificate of Citizenship

If, for some reason, you don't have your child's birth certificate, the SSA will accept a U.S. passport; a religious record made before your child turned five that shows the date of birth; or a U.S. hospital record of birth.

The SSA is also a bit picky about what they will and won't accept as proof of identity. "An acceptable document must be current (not expired) and show your child's name, identifying information, and preferably, a recent photograph."

They may also accept:

- State-issued non-driver identification card
- Adoption decree
- Doctor, hospital, or clinic record
- Religious record
- Daycare or school record
- School identification card

Born Abroad

If your child was born abroad, when you apply for her Social Security number you'll need to bring one of the following:

- Foreign birth certificate
- Certificate of Birth Abroad
- Certificate of Report of Birth
- Consular Report of Birth Abroad
- Certificate of Naturalization
- Passport

APPLYING FOR YOUR OWN SOCIAL SECURITY CARD

Getting a Social Security number for yourself is similar to getting one for your child. To prove your identity, you can show one of the following:

- U.S. driver's license
- State-issued non-driver identification card
- U.S. passport
- Employee identification card
- School identification card
- Health insurance card (*not* Medicaid)
- U.S. military identification card
- Life insurance policy

They'll want to see the original documents, so don't bother bringing photocopies; they won't be accepted.

There's no cost for getting a Social Security number and card. The SSA warns, "If someone contacts you and wants to charge you for getting a number or card, please remember that these Social Security services are free. You can report anyone attempting to charge you by calling our Office of the Inspector General hotline at 1-800-269-0271."

WHAT TO DO IF YOU'RE A NONCITIZEN

About the only noncitizens needing Social Security numbers are those authorized to work in the United States by the Department of Homeland Security. For example, noncitizens who are in the United States on a student visa generally don't need a Social Security card to do many of the things American citizens do—get a driver's license or register for school, for instance.

If you need an SSN, you can apply in your home country before coming to the United States or, having arrived in America, you can visit your local SSA office. The first is the easier option.

When you visit the SSA, you'll need your paperwork showing that you're authorized to work in the United States. The SSA recommends you wait until ten days after arriving in the United States to make your application, since that will give the agency time to verify your documents from the Department of Homeland Security. You'll also need:

- Two documents verifying your identity, immigration status, and age.
- A completed Application for a Social Security Card (Form SS-5), which you can download from the SSA's website.

As usual, the documents must be original and not photocopies. You can't use one document as two forms of identification; the best and easiest forms are your birth certificate and passport.

If you hold a J-1 or J-2 exchange visa, the SSA will want to see your Certificate of Eligibility for Exchange Visitor Status (Form DS-2019). If you're a student holding a J-1 visa, you'll have to provide the SSA with a letter from your sponsor on the sponsor's letterhead, including an original signature. The letter should authorize you to work in the United States.

If you are an international student with an F-1 or M-1 visa, the SSA will need to see your Certificate of Eligibility for Nonimmigrant Student Status (Form I-20).

You'll receive your Social Security card in the mail.

REPLACING A LOST OR STOLEN CARD

If your card disappears it's *extremely important* that you report the loss and get a replacement card as soon as possible. Identify theft is among the most widespread crimes being practiced today, and as mentioned earlier, Social Security numbers are widely used as a form of identification. You're only allowed to replace it three times in the course of a year and can only have ten replacement cards over your lifetime.

If you think someone is fraudulently using your card or your child's card, there are several ways to report it:

- Go to www.idtheft.gov
- Call 1-877-438-4338; or TTY: 1-866-653-4261

my Social Security

If you want to apply for a replacement card (or check the amount of your monthly benefits, should you retire right now), the Social Security Administration has set up a website called *my* Social Security (www .ssa.gov/myaccount). You can go to this site and set up an account, and it will guide you through the steps you need to take. However, this online service is available only if you're from certain states.

You can use *my* Social Security to get a replacement card if you:

- Are a U.S. citizen, eighteen years or older, with a U.S. mailing address
- Are *only* requesting a replacement card (not a name change)

- Have a valid driver's license or state-issued ID card from one of the following:

  - District of Columbia (driver's license only)
  - Iowa
  - Kentucky
  - Michigan
  - Nebraska
  - New Mexico
  - Washington
  - Wisconsin (driver's license only)

CHANGING YOUR NAME

If you legally change your name when you get married, divorced, or for some other reason, you will have to change your name on your Social Security card. This is important because the government has to ensure that your earnings are properly tracked to credit your benefits. It would be really bad if, because you neglected to change your name in the SSA's records, five or ten years of your working life was credited to the wrong benefit account.

Fortunately, changing your name with the SSA isn't difficult.

Married or Divorced

If you've recently married, and have changed your name, go to a SSA office with the marriage certificate as well as a document proving your previous identity (an expired driver's license will work fine). If you've recently divorced, and changed your name, bring a copy of the divorce decree and a document proving your new name.

Adoption or Naturalization

If you have been adopted or have recently become a naturalized citizen, bring an adoption degree or Certificate of Naturalization. As well, bring two documents identifying you by your old name and by your new name.

PROTECTING YOUR SOCIAL SECURITY NUMBER

Guard Against Identity Theft

Social Security numbers (SSNs) are among the most widely used forms of identification in the United States. You use them to get everything from a driver's license to a credit card. For that reason, protecting your Social Security number is extremely important.

IDENTITY THEFT IN THE UNITED STATES

Particularly with the expansion of the Internet and the growth of sophisticated computer systems, identity theft in the United States has skyrocketed. A U.S. Department of Justice study concluded that in 2012, identity theft accounted for about $24.7 billion in losses. That's nearly double the $14 billion in other property crimes. Another analysis suggests that one in three Americans has been the victim of identity fraud. Bureau of Justice Statistics report that in 2014, 17.6 million U.S. residents experienced identity theft.

Students and Identity Theft

Many college students are victims of identity theft, partly because they are at the age when they start to obtain credit cards. Also, the practice of having grades posted by Social Security number is one way in which their identity is often stolen. This gives thieves a list of valid SSNs they can exploit.

All of these statistics suggest the importance of protecting your identity, particularly your Social Security number. The SSA and other organizations have many suggestions about the best ways to do this. Here are a few:

Don't Carry Your Social Security Card with You

There's no reason at all for you to carry your Social Security card around in your wallet. It can be stolen; you could lose your wallet or leave it somewhere. Your Social Security card is extremely important, and you should not treat it carelessly.

Leave it at home, preferably somewhere safe and secure where you keep other important documents. To keep it really safe, rent a safe-deposit box at your bank and store the card there.

Don't Give Out Your SSN Unless You Have To

There are a relatively limited number of circumstances in which you will have to provide your Social Security number to anyone. If you open a bank account or are applying for a credit card, you'll be asked for it. But there's no reason for most people to know it or want to know it. It's not uncommon for various retailers to ask for the last four digits of your SSN; but be cautious about giving out the full number.

Beware of Unsecured Websites

A huge amount (though not all) of identity theft takes place through the Internet. All of us are so connected, through our smartphones, laptops, and all our other devices that we tend to grow careless about protecting important information like our Social Security numbers.

If a website address begins with https:// (as opposed to http://; the letter *s* is the key here), that indicates that it's a secured site. You should still be cautious about giving out your SSN, but at least on a secured site you will be relatively safe from identity theft.

The Bank Scam

This is a widespread scam that particularly targets elderly people. Your phone rings, and the voice on the other end says he's from your bank. He informs you that there's been some questionable activity in your account. So far, this all sounds normal. This kind of thing happens, and usually the bank will (assuming the suspicious transactions are unauthorized) void your debit/credit card and issue you a new one. But this time, the friendly voice on the other end of the line asks you to "confirm" your account by giving him your Social Security number and your bank account number. Don't do it. The bank doesn't need either of those pieces of information from you. If you're still worried, stop by a branch of the bank and ask the bank manager about the phone call.

In general, it's a good idea not to click on websites unless you have some idea of what they are. Many scammers set up websites that look as if they are legitimate.

The same thing goes for e-mail. If you receive an e-mail from someone you don't know and with a subject line you don't recognize, delete it rather than open it. Many such e-mails are designed to steal your personal information, including your Social Security number.

Get a Shredder

Identity thieves look for documents that contain your Social Security number. With all the stuff that comes in the mail for you, it's not surprising that some of it will have information that identity thieves find valuable. You can deny them access to this sort of information by running your billing receipts, credit card offers, and so on through a shredder. Shredders are cheap, and you can pick one up at your local office supplies store.

Phishing for Numbers

An extremely common online scam technique is called "phishing." Here's how it works: You receive a piece of unsolicited e-mail. It might appear to come from somewhere you know (your bank, for instance); or it might be an enticement that offers you something for nothing ("Click here for thousands of dollars in free quality merchandise!"). If you click on the link and go to the site, you'll be asked to put in various bits of information—your password, your SSN, your address, and so on. The owners of the site want you to give them as much information as possible so they can steal your identity. A good rule of thumb is to be suspicious of unsolicited e-mails and avoid sites with which you're not familiar. And be wary of great offers. If something sounds too good to be true—it probably is.

WHAT TO DO

If, despite your best precautions, you think your Social Security number has been stolen, then you need to take immediate action to prevent serious damage from happening to your accounts and your credit. You should:

- File a police report as soon as you discover the theft. Sadly, identity theft has become extremely common, so police resources are stretched. There is a limited amount the police can do to help you.

But you should still notify them to help protect yourself in the event that someone attempts to use your identity.

- Get in touch with your bank. Inform them that someone has stolen your Social Security number. They'll be on their guard and will monitor your account to make sure there is no suspicious activity. It's possible they may issue you a new debit card.
- Report the theft to one of the three major credit score agencies: Equifax, TransUnion, or Experian. Ask them to place a fraud alert in your file.
- Contact the Internal Revenue Service at www.irs.gov/uac/identity-protection or call them at 1-800-908-4490.
- Get in touch with the Federal Trade Commission at www.idtheft.gov. You can also call 1-877-IDTHEFT.

After doing this, carefully monitor your bank account and credit card accounts. Keep up the monitoring for several months to make sure there's no unauthorized activity. If there is, report it immediately to your bank and the appropriate credit card companies.

Myths about Social Security Numbers

The tinfoil hat crowd on the Internet has spread some strange rumors over the years about Social Security numbers. Foremost among these is the idea that your SSN contains information that identify you to the government. In particular, it's said that the middle two numbers indicate your race. This is untrue. The first three digits are an Area number; the second two are a Group number; and the last four are a Serial number. There are no hidden codes or meanings in any of this.

Your Social Security number is deeply important to maintaining your identity as a U.S. citizen. Never be careless with it.

QUALIFICATIONS FOR RECEIVING BENEFITS

Who's Eligible?

A lot of myths have been passed around the Internet about who's receiving Social Security benefits. Many people, for instance, believe that illegal immigrants, immediately upon arriving in the United States, file for and start getting Social Security benefits. Others suggest that there is massive fraud in the system and that people are getting two, three, or more sets of benefit payments.

While there's unquestionably some degree of fraud practiced in relationship to the system (like any large, complex system Social Security is subject to some degree of fraud), the truth is that the retirement part of Social Security works pretty much the way it's supposed to. Those who paid into the system are the ones who get benefits. Those who didn't, don't.

All U.S. citizens who work in the United States are qualified to receive Social Security benefits. As a worker, every time you receive a paycheck the government deducts money from it to pay for the Social Security system. As mentioned earlier, these deductions, or payroll tax, are marked on your check as FICA, which stands for Federal Insurance Contributions Act.

As it's currently set up, Social Security gives you one credit for every $1,260 you earn. You can earn a maximum of four credits per year, and when you've earned forty credits, you're eligible to start receiving benefits. (Keep in mind that the $1,260 number is adjusted each year to take inflation and other things into account.)

WHO ELSE QUALIFIES?

Assuming you fall into the category of those qualifying for benefits, there are some members of your family who may also be eligible to receive benefits. These include:

- Your spouse, if she or he is sixty-two or older
- Your spouse, if she or he cares for a dependent child who is younger than sixteen or is disabled
- Your children, if you're collecting benefits. The children must be either:

    - Younger than eighteen and not married
    - Disabled
    - Full-time students up to and including the age of nineteen and unmarried

- Dependent grandchildren
- An ex-spouse who is at least sixty-two and retired, hasn't remarried, and to whom you were married at least ten years and have been divorced from for at least two years

Expanding the Definition of Marriage

Like other agencies of the federal government, the Social Security Administration has had to adapt to changing definitions of marriage. In particular, the SSA now recognizes same-sex marriage as qualifying for spousal benefits throughout all fifty states.

When a Breadwinner Dies

There are certain circumstances in which someone can receive Social Security benefits even if he or she isn't yet sixty-two years old. For example, if a family's principal breadwinner dies, then the widow or widower might be eligible to receive Social Security benefits. We'll discuss this more thoroughly in the section of this book that deals with benefits for widows and widowers. For now, just note that this is an aspect of coverage within the Social Security system.

HOW MUCH WILL I GET?

In determining the amount of money to pay a beneficiary, the SSA takes three key things into account:

1. How long you have worked
2. How much you earned
3. How old you are when you decide to start taking benefits

These determinations apply whether you've spent your career being employed by other people or if you have been self-employed for all or part of your working life.

Your Working Life

The Social Security Administration looks at the totality of your working life and asks: What were your top-earning thirty-five years? Note that these need not be consecutive years. If you had significant earnings for ten years, then were unemployed for a couple of years, and then worked again for another twenty-five years, the government will discount the unemployed years.

Who Doesn't Qualify?

Even though most U.S. workers are covered by Social Security, some are not. These include:

- Federal workers who were hired before 1984
- Some state and local workers
- Railroad workers who've worked on the railroads for more than ten years

Still that leaves more than 95 percent of the U.S. workforce covered.

If you didn't work for an entire thirty-five years, the SSA will fill in the empty years with zeros. This is one reason why, especially if your employment over the years has been a bit spotty, it's a good idea to keep working as long as possible.

The years don't have to be those that you worked most recently. The SSA starts from the beginning of your working life, when you first started paying taxes into the system, and goes from there.

Using these top thirty-five years of your career, the SSA creates an average, called the average indexed monthly earnings (AIME). They use this number to determine your primary insurance amount (PIA), which is what your monthly benefit will be once you've reached your full retirement age (FRA). All of this information is encapsulated in your Social Security statement, which we'll talk about shortly.

Your Starting Date

Another important factor that affects the amount of your monthly benefit is when you decide to start taking those benefits.

The earliest age at which you can apply for Social Security benefits is sixty-two. However, this isn't necessarily when you *should* start collecting them. We'll discuss this later in more detail. But for right now, mark age sixty-two as the date you can first start collecting your benefits.

Immigrants

The Social Security Administration reaches out to immigrants in a number of ways:

- By visiting www.ssa.gov/multilanguage/, immigrants who do not know English well can choose from eighteen other languages to read about Social Security.
- Immigrants can request the services of an interpreter, whom the SSA will provide, free of charge.

If you are a foreign student holding an F-1, J-1, or M-1 visa and are working on campus or by a special arrangement with the college or university, your earnings will not be taxed for purposes of Social Security. However, if you have a work visa of a different type, your wages can be taxed for Social Security. For more information about this, go to www.irs.gov/forms-pubs and look for publications 515 and 519. You can also call the Internal Revenue Service directly at 1-800-829-1040.

Of course, if you continue working, especially if you have a reasonably high-earning job, you increase the number of years that can be figured into your AIME and thus, potentially, raise the amount of your benefit. This situation lasts until you reach age seventy. At that point, your AIME is fixed. You can continue to work, of course, but it won't have any effect on increasing your benefit.

YOUR FULL RETIREMENT AGE

When You're Expected to Retire

As discussed earlier, you can start taking your benefits when you turn sixty-two. However, it's usually better to wait until you reach what the Social Security Administration terms your full retirement age (FRA). If you wait until you reach your FRA, you'll receive your full retirement benefit, although you can increase the amount of your benefit even more by waiting until age seventy to file a claim.

DETERMINING YOUR FRA

Congress changed the FRA in 1983. Up to that point, it had been pinned at sixty-five. Since this was the age at which it was anticipated that baby boomers would start to retire in large numbers (and thus start claiming benefits). Congress took several steps to increase the amount of money Social Security was taking in. One step was to increase the payroll tax rate. Another step was to increase the FRA.

The following table indicates how the SSA currently figures full retirement age.

YEAR OF BIRTH	FULL RETIREMENT AGE
1937 or earlier	65 years
1938	65 years 2 months
1939	65 years 4 months
1940	65 years 6 months
1941	65 years 8 months
1942	65 years 10 months

YEAR OF BIRTH	FULL RETIREMENT AGE
1943–54	66 years
1955	66 years 2 months
1956	66 years 4 months
1957	66 years 6 months
1958	66 years 8 months
1959	66 years 10 months
1960 and after	67 years

FIGURING YOUR LIFE EXPECTANCY

When you're determining questions such as when you should begin taking Social Security benefits, the underlying unknown is, How much longer am I going to be alive? Obviously, it's impossible to predict the answer to that with any degree of certainty, but statisticians have given us a pretty good general idea. Their conclusions are reflected in the following table.

AGE	TOTAL YEARS REMAINING	MALE	FEMALE
0	77.9	75.4	80.4
1	77.5	74.9	79.9
5	73.6	71.0	76.0
10	68.6	66.1	71.0
15	63.7	61.1	66.1
20	58.8	56.4	61.2
25	54.1	51.8	56.3
30	49.4	47.1	51.5
35	44.6	42.5	46.7
40	39.9	37.8	41.9
45	35.4	33.3	37.2

AGE	TOTAL YEARS REMAINING	MALE	FEMALE
50	30.9	29.0	32.7
55	26.7	24.9	28.2
60	22.5	20.9	23.9
65	18.6	17.2	19.9
70	15.0	13.7	16.0
75	11.7	10.6	12.5
80	8.8	7.9	9.4
85	6.5	5.8	6.8
90	4.6	4.1	4.8
95	3.2	2.9	3.3
100	2.3	2.1	2.3

Clearly there are lots of factors involved, and this chart is pretty simple. For a more sophisticated and complex calculation, go to www.livingto100.com.

The purpose of this examination is to figure out whether or not you should take early benefits—that is, start collecting them before you reach your FRA. In general, you're trying to determine what financial planners call a "break-even point." You do this by comparing the differing amounts you'll get from Social Security, depending on when you claim benefits and how long you live after that. If you claim benefits early but don't live to your break-even age, then you made the right decision to claim early. If you claim later and live longer, you again made the right decision, since your benefit will be larger than if you'd claimed early. The bad decision is to claim early and then live up to or past your break-even age. That's the point at which you've left money on the table and may even have financial difficulties because of the smaller size of your benefit. In subsequent chapters we'll discuss more details of taking early benefits versus claiming later.

GETTING STARTED WITH SOCIAL SECURITY

What You Need to Know

Although it's pretty easy to apply for benefits, the Social Security Administration recommends that you apply three months before you want your benefits to start coming. They strongly urge you to apply online rather than in person.

"In most cases, once your application is submitted electronically, you're done. There are no forms to sign and usually no documentation is required. Social Security will process your application and contact you if any further information is required."

—Social Security Administration

You can use the online application if you're at least sixty-one years and nine months old, are not currently receiving benefits, haven't already applied for benefits (say, at a regional SSA office), and don't want benefits to start any later than four months from the time you apply.

You can apply online on the Social Security Administration's website, www.ssa.gov/onlineservices/. The SSA's online hours of operation are Monday through Friday 5 A.M. to 1 A.M.; Saturday from 5 A.M. to 11 P.M.; and Sunday from 8 A.M. to 11:30 P.M.

OTHER WAYS TO APPLY

There are two other ways to apply for benefits: over the phone and in person.

Applying in Person
You probably don't want to sit around at the SSA office, patiently waiting for the long line of people ahead of you to finish their business. However, you can significantly cut down on your wait time by making an appointment ahead of time. Call 1-800-772-1213 and set up a time to talk to someone. Particularly if you're unsure or insecure about parts of the process, this is a good route to go.

Applying over the Phone
To apply over the phone, call 1-800-772-1213 Monday through Friday between 7 A.M. and 7 P.M. However, be aware that the phone lines are likely to be busy early in the morning and will be especially busy early in the week and the month. So be ready to sit on hold for quite a while.

WHAT SHOULD YOU KNOW?

Before applying, whether online, over the phone, or in person, there are certain basic things you should know:

1. **Your full retirement age.** You can learn this from the table in the previous chapter. Generally speaking, it will be between sixty-six and sixty-seven. You need to know this even if you're applying for benefits before reaching your FRA.

2. **When you can start receiving benefits.** You can start taking benefits any time after turning sixty-two or as late as age seventy. Remember that if you take early benefits (that is, take them before reaching your FRA), you will not receive your full benefits. If you wait until you reach age seventy, your benefit will be larger than if you start taking it at your FRA.

3. **How working during retirement can affect your benefits.** We'll discuss this important question shortly.

4. **Delayed retirement credits.** We'll talk about these in the next section.

5. **Your life expectancy.** Look this up on the table in the previous chapter.

Retirement Estimator

The Social Security Administration has very kindly provided a Retirement Estimator to calculate how much your benefits will be at different ages. You can access the Retirement Estimator at www.ssa.gov/retire/estimator.html.

Delayed Retirement Credits

If you choose to begin taking your Social Security benefit some time after you've reached and passed your full retirement age, your benefits increase. The longer you delay, the greater the increase, until you reach age seventy. At that point, the additional increases stop. You can continue to work, of course, but it won't make a difference in the size of your benefits.

The following table, taken from the SSA's website, shows the rate of increase for people born in different years. If you were born January 1, refer to the rate of increase for the previous year.

INCREASE FOR DELAYED RETIREMENT		
Year of Birth	Yearly Rate of Increase	Monthly Rate of Increase
1933–34	5.5%	11/24 of 1%
1935–36	6%	1/2 of 1%
1937–38	6.5%	13/24 of 1%
1939–40	7%	7/12 of 1%
1941–42	7.5%	5/8 of 1%
1943 or later	8%	2/3 of 1%

Retroactive Benefits

Here's an important note from the SSA: "If you've already reached full retirement age, you can choose to start receiving benefits before the month you apply. However, we cannot pay retroactive benefits for any month before you reached full retirement age or more than 6 months in the past."

This is particularly useful if you're past your FRA but have an urgent need for a lump sum of cash, perhaps for a medical emergency. For example, David has decided that rather than beginning his benefits at age sixty-seven, his FRA, he will delay taking them until he reaches age seventy. However, at age sixty-nine he develops an illness that requires a lengthy operation. Not all the cost will be covered by his insurance, so he decides to apply for retroactive Social Security benefits. David receives a delayed retirement credit (DRC) for the two years he's past his FRA. Unfortunately, he can only receive six months' worth of benefits, but all the same the lump sum he receives goes a long way toward paying some of the bills for his operation.

THE DOCUMENTS YOU'LL NEED

To file for Social Security benefits, you have to have a sizeable amount of information about yourself, backed up with original documents. The part about "original" is important; the SSA will *not* accept photocopies of your birth certificate and other documentation.

Lost Your Birth Certificate?

If you've lost your birth certificate or never had a copy of it in the first place, the state and city of your birth will be able to provide it to you. Go to city hall in the city or town in which you were born and ask for a copy. You'll have to provide photo ID (your driver's license is sufficient) and pay a small fee to cover the costs of the transaction.

Documents you'll need include:

- Birth certificate or other proof of birth
- Proof of U.S. citizenship; if you're an alien legally residing in the United States, proof of your legal status
- If you're a veteran who served before 1968, a copy of your military service papers
- Copies of your W-2 forms; if you work for more than one employer, W-2s from each of them
- If you're self-employed, a copy of your most recent tax return
- If you're married to the chief breadwinner in the household, your marriage certificate

ESTIMATING YOUR BENEFITS

How Much Are You Going to Get?

You need to take Social Security benefits into account as an important part of your financial picture for retirement. When you begin to draw up your retirement budget, though, you need a clearer idea of exactly how much those benefits might be.

The two factors that determine this are:

1. How much have you earned?
2. When do you intend to start taking benefits?

The first step in determining what the answer to those questions might be comes in the form of your Social Security statement.

The Check Is *Not* in the Mail

One significant change from past practices is that the SSA no longer mails out actual physical checks every month to those taking benefits. Since 2011, the SSA has required that recipients of benefits receive their money through electronic transfer to their bank accounts. Therefore, when you sign up for Social Security benefits, you'll have to provide some information about your bank account (specifically, the routing number, which is the number at the bottom left-hand corner of your check). You also have the option—if you don't have a bank account or don't want to give the SSA information about it—of using a prepaid debit card. Each month, the amount of your benefit is automatically loaded on the card, and you use it to make purchases, just as you would a regular bank debit card.

YOUR STATEMENT

Between ages twenty-five and sixty, the Social Security Administration mails your statement to you every five years. When you hit the magic age of sixty, you'll start receiving your statement every year.

What's on Your Statement?

The statement you receive will contain three things:

1. Your estimated benefit
2. Your year-by-year earnings that the system used to estimate your benefit
3. An explanation of how the SSA uses the information it has gathered to calculate your benefit

Estimated Benefit

In the top right-hand corner of the first page of the statement is your estimated benefit at your full retirement age. Inside, the statement tells you:

- Whether you've earned enough credits to qualify for retirement benefits
- What your retirement benefits would be if you retired at your FRA, if you retired at age sixty-two, and what they'd be if you retired at age seventy
- Whether you've earned enough credits to qualify for disability benefits and, if you are disabled right now, what your monthly benefit would be
- Whether your spouse and children would qualify for survivors benefits in the event of your death, and what those monthly

benefits would be (this is broken down by child and spouse caring for the child, as well as spouse if she or he started taking those benefits at your FRA)

- The limit on total family survivors benefits
- Whether you have enough credits to qualify for Medicare

Let's look, briefly, at the statement of Marilyn, who turned sixty-two several months previously. She examines her statement and sees that she's earned enough credits to take Social Security benefits. She can get $1,429 a month if she claims her benefits now. However, if she waits five years until her full retirement age of sixty-seven, her benefits increase to $2,006 per month (an increase of almost 29 percent). Further, if she can wait until she turns seventy to claim, her benefits rise to $2,787, an increase of 28 percent over the amount she would get by claiming at her FRA, and an increase of almost 49 percent over what she would get by claiming now. Sensibly, Marilyn decides to wait at least until she reaches her FRA. At that point she can re-evaluate the situation and see if she wants to wait until age seventy. (This, of course, is where the issue of life expectancy kicks in. If Marilyn's family has a history of living many years, it makes sense to wait the longer time. If they tend to die earlier, she may want to put in her claim at her FRA or even, depending on her life expectancy, at the early age of sixty-two.)

Year-by-Year Earnings Record

This is a table on your statement. It shows how much taxable income you earned for each of the thirty-five years that Social Security averaged to come up with your estimated benefit. You may notice that some years are marked with zeros. Those were years in which you had no taxable income. The longer you work, the more of those zeros will go away and be replaced by income numbers, and the higher your estimated benefit will be.

If you earned more than $118,500 in a given year, that's all the taxable income the statement will show (even though you may have actually earned quite a bit more). That's because $118,500 is the upper limit on income taxable for Social Security.

At the bottom of the table are the totals of tax paid by you and your employer toward Social Security and Medicare.

Marilyn's work history shows considerable variation in her taxable income. For seven years, she had none, so these years appear as zero. On the other hand, in one year her taxable income rose to more than $80,000. For the past few years, her taxable income has remained relatively steady. Marilyn knows that her situation will be improved if she can replace those zeros with some numbers. Working past her FRA until she turns seventy will do that, giving her an increased benefit.

Medicare Cap versus Social Security Cap

Although there is a cap on Social Security taxable earnings ($118,500), that is not true of Medicare. The maximum taxable amount for Medicare began increasing in 1991, and since 1994 there has been no cap on earnings that are taxable to pay for the program.

Explanation of Social Security

The third part of your statement explains in some detail how Social Security works. Topics it takes up include:

- Retirement benefits
- Disability benefits

- Family benefits
- Survivors benefits
- Extra help with Medicare
- Working while receiving benefits

The section has extensive links (if looking at your statement online) to resources as well as phone numbers to call for assistance and information.

my Social Security

If you want to look at your statement or get other information about your benefits, the best thing is to set up a *my* Social Security account. To set it up, go to www.ssa.gov/myaccount. The site will allow you to access your statement any time you want.

If you find an error in your statement, it's important to draw it to the attention of the SSA immediately so that it can be corrected. If you feel your earnings were misreported for a particular year, find your W-2 for that year and have it in hand when you call the SSA at 1-800-772-1213.

DISABILITY BENEFITS

When You Can't Work Anymore

No one gets up in the morning and says, "I think I'll be injured today so I can't work anymore." Disability is something that is difficult, if not impossible, to plan for accurately. You don't know if or when it's going to happen and what sort of financial assistance you'll need. And the fact is, it's more common than we tend to think. It's estimated that a twenty-year-old worker has a one-in-four chance of becoming disabled before she or he reaches full retirement age. The Social Security Administration's statistics show that in 2015 the agency received 2.4 million applications for disability benefits; of those, the SSA awarded benefits in more than 775,000 cases. Currently about 8.9 million workers receive disability payments.

Like other aspects of your financial planning, Social Security is not the sole answer to the financial issues of being unable to work. Nonetheless, Social Security disability benefits can be a big help in coping with something that's personally and professionally devastating.

SOCIAL SECURITY DISABILITY INSURANCE (SSDI)

The government pays two kinds of disability benefits: SSDI and Supplemental Security Income (SSI). We'll deal with SSI in a separate section. We'll also talk later about Social Security's plans for children who suffer from disabilities. For now, let's concentrate on SSDI.

The SSA explains its disabilities program in this way:

Social Security pays benefits to people who can't work because they have a medical condition that's expected to last at least one year or result in death. While some programs give money to people with partial disability or short-term disability, Social Security does not.

Earnings Tests

To determine whether or not you're eligible for Social Security disability benefits, you must consider two earnings tests:

1. A recent work test
2. A duration of work test

For the recent work test, the SSA offers the following table:

RULES FOR WORK NEEDED FOR THE RECENT WORK TEST	
IF YOU BECAME DISABLED:	**THEN, YOU GENERALLY NEED:**
In or before the quarter you turned 24	1.5 years of work during the 3-year period ending with the quarter your disability began.
In the quarter after you turned age 24 but before the quarter you turned 31	Work during half the time for the period beginning with the quarter after you turned 21 and ending with the quarter you became disabled. Example: If you became disabled in the quarter you turned age 27, then you would need 3 years of work out of the 6-year period ending with the quarter you became disabled.
In the quarter you turned age 31 or later	Work during 5 years out of the 10-year period ending with the quarter your disability began.

The SSA also provides a table to determine where you stand on the work test:

EXAMPLES OF WORK NEEDED FOR THE DURATION OF WORK TEST	
IF YOU BECOME DISABLED:	**THEN YOU GENERALLY NEED:**
Before age 28	1.5 years of work
Age 30	2 years
Age 34	3 years
Age 38	3 years
Age 42	5 years
Age 44	5.5 years
Age 46	6 years
Age 48	6.5 years
Age 50	7 years
Age 52	7.5 years
Age 54	8 years
Age 56	8.5 years
Age 58	9 years
Age 60	9.5 years

APPLYING FOR
DISABILITY BENEFITS

You can apply for disability benefits the same three ways as you can for retirement benefits: by phone, in person, or online. The SSA warns that processing time for an application can take anywhere from three to five months, so it's important to start the application process as soon as you're able.

To apply, you'll need the following documentation:

- Social Security number
- Birth certificate
- Names, addresses, and phone numbers of the medical personnel who took care of you and the dates on which you received care
- Names and dosages of prescription medicine you take
- Medical records from the treatment you're receiving; this includes doctors, therapists, hospitals, and clinics
- Laboratory and test results
- Proof of where you worked and what kind of work you did
- A recent W-2; if you're self-employed, your most recent tax return

Sadly, this being the government after all, you'll spend quite a lot of time filling out forms. Keep going, though. This is very important to your financial well-being.

If You've Committed a Crime

If you have an outstanding warrant for your arrest or if you've been convicted of a crime, you must let the Social Security Administration know. You can't receive disability benefits during the time you're in jail, but your eligible family members can continue to receive their benefits.

Deciding If You're Really Disabled

After you've completed your application it goes to the Disability Determination Services (DDS) in your state for consideration. These folks will contact your doctors or other caregivers to find out more details of your medical condition. It's possible you may have to go for a special examination, either by your doctor or one picked by the DDS. In the end, the DDS makes its recommendation to the SSA about whether to grant your application based on five questions:

1. Are you working?
2. Is your medical condition "severe"?
3. Does your condition match an SSA listing for disability?
4. Can you do the type of work you did before?
5. Can you do any other kind of work?

This last point is crucial and is a reason many disability claims are disallowed. Even if you're unable to perform the kind of work you did before you suffered the disability, it's possible you may have the education, training, or physical skills to do something else. If that's the case, your claim will probably be denied.

The SSA will notify you by letter of the resolution of your claim. If the claim's been approved, the letter will tell you how much money you'll get per month and when payments will start.

Benefits to Dependents

If you are the principle breadwinner in your family and you become disabled, your spouse may be entitled to benefits. To receive these benefits your husband or wife must be at least sixty-two years old or must be caring for your child, who must be under sixteen years old.

Appealing a Denial
If your claim is denied and you disagree with the reason (outlined in the letter from the SSA), you have the right to appeal the decision.

Appealing a decision by the SSA for the denial of SSDI benefits is the same as any other SSA appeals process. We'll discuss in detail a bit later how the SSA appeals process works.

FAMILY DISABILITY BENEFITS

Because the government understands that your disability also affects members of your family, it's possible to obtain benefits for them as well. These include:

- Your spouse, if she or he is sixty-two or older
- Your spouse, if she or he is caring for your child and the child is younger than sixteen or disabled
- Your unmarried child younger than eighteen
- Your child eighteen or older if she or he has a disability that began before the child reached the age of twenty-two

Other Benefits and Disability

It's possible for other benefits to be affected by your disability benefits. We'll discuss this in more detail in the respective chapters that cover the Windfall Elimination Provision and the Government Pension Offset.

TICKET TO WORK

If you're eighteen through sixty-four years of age and qualify for disability benefits, the Social Security Administration offers you a program called Ticket to Work. Its object is to train you, free of cost, in skills that can lead to employment. The SSA explains:

> When you take part in the Ticket to Work program, you can get help finding a job, vocational rehabilitation, or other support. Employment networks and state vocational rehabilitation agencies provide these services. These networks include private organizations and government agencies that have agreed to work with Social Security. They provide employment services and other support to beneficiaries with disabilities.

If you want to apply to participate in the program, you can call the Ticket to Work Help Line at 1-866-968-7842 or visit the website at www.ssa.gov/work.

SUPPLEMENTAL SECURITY INCOME

Adding to Your Disability Benefits

As you can see from the previous chapter, the Social Security Administration is careful in its definition both of "disabilities" and who qualifies for disability benefits. These benefits are the primary way in which the system assists workers who, for one reason or another, are unable to work. In this chapter, we'll talk about a second kind of disability benefits: Supplemental Security Income (SSI).

WHERE DID IT COME FROM?

The original 1935 act that created Social Security also mandated state programs of Aid to the Blind, Old-Age Assistance, and Aid to the Permanently and Totally Disabled. In the 1970s, the Nixon administration decided to federalize and centralize these programs under the umbrella of the SSA. The result was a 1972 amendment creating SSI. The program began in 1974.

Differently Funded

Unlike Social Security, which is primarily funded by a payroll tax (FICA), the SSI is funded out of general Treasury revenues, which come from income tax, corporate taxes, and other sources.

As of August 2014 SSI benefits were going to 8.3 million people, 1.3 million of whom were under the age of eighteen. These numbers, and the amount of dollars being doled out by the program, continue to increase. This represents a challenge to the government, since SSI isn't funded the same way as Social Security and therefore isn't subject to the same kinds of fixes we discussed earlier.

Disabled but Working

If you are disabled but are still working, any money you spend on items you need because you're disabled (e.g., a wheelchair, crutches, special transportation) is deducted from the SSA's calculation of your income. Under the same logic, the SSA deducts from the income calculation any money a blind person uses to do her or his work.

WHO'S ELIGIBLE?

The key determinants for whether or not you qualify for SSI are your age and your income. In calculating your income, the Social Security Administration does *not* count the following:

- The first $20 in income you receive each month from all sources
- The first $65 you earn in a month as wages and half of your earnings over $65 received in a month
- Supplemental Nutrition Assistance Program (SNAP) benefits
- Most home energy assistance

Part of your spouse's income is included in the calculation; if you're under eighteen, the SSA uses part of your parents' income in calculating your income. To qualify for SSI benefits, your income must be less than $733 per month if you're an individual ($1,100 for couples). Note that these figures are as of 2016 and change from year to year. For the latest information on this, go to www.ssa.gov/ssi/.

In addition to income, the SSA includes in its means test your resources (that is, assets you own, as opposed to money you earn):

- Real estate (but not, it's important to note, your primary home)
- Cash
- Bonds
- Stocks
- Savings

The SSA doesn't count as part of your resources your car, insurance policies worth less than $1,500, and burial plots you own. If your resources total $2,000 or less ($3,000 for a couple), you may be eligible for SSI.

HOW IS YOUR BENEFIT CALCULATED?

After the Social Security Administration has calculated your countable income, excluding the various things listed in the preceding section, it subtracts this number from the benefit amount (currently $733 for individuals).

Let's take a for instance: John is sixty-three and suffers from diabetes, which makes him no longer able to work at his lifelong job. His

Social Security benefit is $400 per month. This counts as income, but the SSA deducts the first $20 of it: $400 – $20 = $380. Now the SSA subtracts $380 from the current SSI benefit: $733 – $380 = $353. John is eligible to receive a monthly SSI benefit of $353. By applying for and receiving SSI benefits, he's come close to doubling his monthly income.

Now let's look at a slightly more complicated example. Emily, sixty-four, is still working part-time but suffers from a disability. Her monthly wage is $317. She applies for SSI benefits. First the SSA subtracts $20 from her wages, since they count it as income: $317 – $20 = $297. Next, the agency subtracts the first $65 of her earned wages: $297 – $65 = $232. Finally, since $232 is more than 65, Emily's countable income is divided in half: $232 ÷ 2 = $116, so $232 – $116 = $116. The SSA now subtracts that from the current benefit amount for individuals: $733 – $116 = $617. This means Emily will receive an SSI monthly benefit of $617. That's in addition to any money she's receiving from Social Security, if she's already put in for benefits.

Mentally Ill Straining Social Security

In a 2006 book, *Disability Rights and the American Social Safety Net*, Jennifer L. Erkulwater argues that one of the main drivers of the increase in disability claims is mental illness, particularly among the young. "Between 1989 and 2001, the proportion of children with a mental impairment grew more than five-fold, increasing from only 6 percent of all children receiving SSI to 32 percent. Today, children and adults with mental disorders outnumber beneficiaries in all other diagnostic categories."

As a further qualification for SSI, you must live in the United States or the Northern Mariana Islands. You must also be a U.S. citizen.

HOW TO APPLY FOR SSI

The process for applying for SSI is the same as that for applying for disability benefits. The list of materials you should bring is similar. You will need:

- Birth certificate
- Social Security card (or other proof of your SSN)
- A mortgage if you own your own home; if you rent, a signed lease
- Information about your income, such as payroll slips, insurance policies, etc.
- Contact information for doctors, hospitals, and clinics where your disability has been treated
- Proof of citizenship
- Your checkbook or some other document that includes your bank account number

SNAP and SSI

If you're eligible for SSI, you may get additional financial assistance through the Supplemental Nutrition Assistance Program (SNAP), formerly known as food stamps. You can sign up for this program at a SSA office, or you can go online at www.fns.usda.gov/snap.

CHILDREN WITH DISABILITIES

Protecting Your Offspring

If you're the parent of a child with disabilities, you know how challenging life can be. In addition to helping your child fully realize her or his potential in an often-challenging world, there is often significant financial pressure on your family. Fortunately, Social Security and Supplemental Security Income can help ease some of this burden.

IF YOU BECAME DISABLED IN CHILDHOOD

If you were disabled when you were younger than age twenty-two and are now an adult, you might be eligible for Social Security Disability Insurance (SSDI). You can qualify for these benefits if either of these circumstances is true:

- At least one of your parents is receiving Social Security benefits; these can either be retirement or disability benefits
- At least one of your parents has died and had worked enough years to qualify for benefits

The key here is that as the "child," you don't need to have worked to receive the benefits. It's sufficient that one or both of your parents were qualified to receive them. Essentially, you piggyback onto your parents' benefits.

IF YOU'RE THE PARENT OF A DISABLED CHILD

Your child may qualify for Supplemental Security Income if she or he is younger than eighteen and has a disability that meets Social Security's definition. As well, your family's income and resources have to fall below the limits set by the Social Security Administration. As previously explained, this is because SSI is designed specifically for those people who have low incomes and scarce resources.

Results May Vary

Even though the federal SSI benefit is the same, the amount your child receives may vary from state to state, since many states supplement SSI payments.

The rules for income and resources are:

- Your child can't be working and earning more than $1,130 a month
- Whatever disability your child has must "severely" limit his or her activities
- The disability must have been or be expected to last at least twelve months or result in death

Applying for Disability Benefits for Your Child

Just as you would if you were applying for disability benefits for yourself, you'll need to supply the SSA with very thorough information about your child's medical condition. They'll want permission from you to talk to your offspring's doctors, therapists, and teachers to determine the nature and extent of the disability. Be prepared to supply medical and school records. Just as with other kinds of disability benefits, this information is passed on to the Disability Determination Services office. The staff there will conduct the actual interviews with the people treating your child. It's possible they may ask your child to undergo an independent medical examination.

Immediate Payments

Even though, as with other benefits, it can take between three and five months to make a determination as to whether your child is eligible for disability benefits, SSI will, for certain conditions, begin payments immediately. These conditions include:

- HIV
- Total blindness
- Total deafness
- Cerebral palsy
- Down syndrome
- Muscular dystrophy
- Severe intellectual disability
- Low birth weight (below two pounds ten ounces)

Even if the SSI ultimately decides against granting benefits, you don't have to pay this money back.

DISABILITY REVIEWS

Because some disabilities change over time, the Social Security Administration will regularly review your child's medical condition.

If the child is expected to improve and is under eighteen, the review will occur once every three years. For low-birth-weight babies, the review will occur around their first birthday. At these reviews, you'll be expected to show that the disability continues to interfere with your child's ability to function normally.

When the child turns eighteen, the SSA conducts a further review, using adult disability rules.

IF YOUR CHILD WANTS TO WORK

Many children, as they grow into their teenage years, want to take a job to earn extra money or help support their families. SSA encourages this. For instance, the agency doesn't count most of your child's income when making the determination as to whether she or he is eligible for SSI benefits. If the child is below age twenty-two and attends school regularly, the SSA excludes $1,780 of their monthly income in their calculations.

PASS

The Social Security Administration runs a program designed to help people with disabilities save money toward fulfilling a work goal. The program is called Plan to Achieve Self-Support (PASS). Once you determine what your work goal is (something you can do with the help of a vocational rehabilitation counselor), contact the SSA office and get a PASS form to fill out. A PASS counselor will work with you on achieving your goal. You must save the money from income other than your SSI benefits, but the SSA may increase SSI benefits once you enroll in PASS. The program is open to disabled children and adults fifteen years or older.

MEDICARE

We'll discuss the government health programs Medicare and Medicaid in much more detail later on. For now, suffice it to say that your disabled child can get immediate help from Medicare if she or he:

- Has chronic renal disease and needs a kidney transplant or maintenance dialysis
- Has Lou Gehrig's disease (amyotrophic lateral sclerosis)

Other Healthcare

The Social Security Act contains a provision for Children with Special Health Care Needs. Under this provision, the SSA administers a series of healthcare programs. The SSI will refer you to them if your child is eligible for benefits. Even if she or he isn't eligible, the programs may be able to help you.

SPOUSAL BENEFITS

A Key Element of Social Security Claims

One of the most important features of the Social Security system is that it works for both you and your spouse. This can be the case even if your husband or wife never paid into the system.

To qualify for spousal benefits, you must be at least sixty-two and have been married to the principal breadwinner in the family for at least a year.

There are some exceptions to this last rule: If your spouse and you have been married to each other for less than a year but she or he is the biological parent of your child, the spouse qualifies for benefits. No matter what your age, you can receive spousal benefits if you're caring for your partner's child.

Divorced?

If you have been divorced from your spouse for at least ten years, you may be eligible for Social Security benefits. We'll discuss this in detail later on.

WHETHER TO FILE

Although your spouse may be eligible for spousal benefits, she shouldn't take them if her own benefit, which is based on her own work history, would be larger. Clearly, her (and your) objective should be to get the largest benefit possible. There are a variety of strategies to do this. Before we discuss them, though, we'll talk briefly about one strategy that no longer exists: file and suspend.

File and Suspend

Under previous Social Security rules, it was possible to file for benefits and then suspend them—that is, not take them—when you reached FRA. Once you did this your spouse could then apply only for spousal benefits (based on your work history). Meanwhile, your benefits would grow because you suspended them. Ideally, your spouse would take spousal benefits until you both reached age seventy, at which time both you and your spouse would take your own full benefits. Thus, rather than waiting to draw income from Social Security, one spouse would receive benefits while both of your benefits would grow.

This file and suspend strategy wasn't used by large numbers of people, mostly because they weren't aware of it. However, it began growing in popularity. At that point, the federal government decided to step in. In 2015 Congress passed a law that ended file and suspend as a viable option.

A similar, but not identical, strategy was also closed off in 2015. If you were born after January 1, 1954, you are no longer allowed to file what is called a restricted application—that is to apply *only* for spousal benefits. The object of this strategy was to file just for your spousal benefits. Because you delay taking your retirement benefits, your own benefits would grow. Then, when you reached age seventy, you would drop the spousal benefit and take your full benefit instead. It was a nice strategy, but sadly you're not allowed to use it anymore—unless your birthday comes before January 1, 1954.

APPLYING FOR SPOUSAL BENEFITS

When applying for these benefits, you will need proof of your marriage and its date to establish that you've been married at least a year (a marriage certificate is fine). You'll also need proof of your age.

Same-Sex Marriage

As of June 2015, the date of the Supreme Court's ruling in *Obergefell v. Hodges*, same-sex marriage became legal in all states of the union. As a consequence, those within such a marriage can now apply for Social Security benefits. In fact, the SSA had granted such benefits to same-sex couples even before *Obergefell v. Hodges* but only in states where same-sex marriage was legal.

In those states that recognize common-law marriage the SSA will treat you as if you're married, and you can file for spousal benefits. Currently the states recognizing common-law marriage are:

- Alabama
- Colorado
- District of Columbia
- Georgia (if created before 1/1/1997)
- Idaho (if created before 1/1/1996)
- Iowa
- Kansas
- Montana
- Ohio (if created before 10/10/1991)
- Oklahoma (if created before 11/1/1998)
- Pennsylvania (if created before 1/1/2005)
- Rhode Island

- South Carolina
- Texas
- Utah

Primary Insurance Amount (PIA)

At this point we need to reintroduce a term: primary insurance amount (PIA), which is the total amount of money a beneficiary is eligible to receive once she or he reaches full retirement age (FRA). This is important here because your spousal benefit can't exceed 50 percent of your partner's PIA. For instance, if Janet's PIA is $2,700 and her husband, Roger, decides to take spousal benefits, the highest such benefits can be is $1,350 (since $2,700 ÷ 2 = $1,350).

However, even though your spousal benefit can be up to 50 percent of your partner's PIA, it doesn't have to be that much. For one thing, if you claim spousal benefits before reaching your full retirement age, the amount will be reduced for each month before your FRA (the exception to this is if the partner claiming the spousal benefits is taking care of your child and the child is under age sixteen).

The following table shows reductions in the 50 percent benefit depending how early you claim it.

AGE	PERCENTAGE OF PARTNER'S BENEFIT
65	45.8%
64	41.7%
63	37.5%
62	35%

As you can see, it pays to wait until reaching your full retirement age to claim spousal benefits—just as it does with your full retirement benefits. However, and this is an important difference, unlike your full retirement benefit, your spousal benefit does *not* increase if you wait to claim it until you're seventy years old. It can never go above that 50 percent of your partner's full benefit. On the other hand, if the partner taking full benefits waits until she or he turns seventy to claim, that 50 percent can be a significantly larger sum of money.

Use a Calculator

The Social Security Administration has a calculator to help give you a rough idea of what your spousal benefits would be. Go to www.ssa.gov/oact/quickcalc/spouse.html.

SURVIVORS BENEFITS

Living after the Breadwinner Is Gone

Few things are more devastating than the death of a family member, no matter whether it is unexpected or has been anticipated for some time. Apart from the emotional loss, there is often a significant financial impact, particularly if the deceased had been the family's primary breadwinner.

Social Security was designed to help prevent families from slipping into poverty. Survivors benefits are an important way in which Social Security fulfills this function.

WHO'S ELIGIBLE?

Those in your family who may be eligible for survivors benefits include your widow or widower, children, and dependent parents. If you are divorced, your divorced spouse may be eligible.

For Social Security to pay these benefits, you must have worked at least ten years. In somewhat macabre fashion, the fewer the number of years you work beyond those ten, the greater will be the possible benefits paid to your survivors. The logic, of course, is that they had anticipated you working for many years more and are therefore more dependent on the money you would have earned.

Illness Before Dying

If, as often happens, you suffered from an illness before your death, it probably limited your ability to work. If, in the three years immediately preceding your death, you were only able to work one and a half years, the Social Security Administration will still pay benefits to your children and your widow or widower if she or he is looking after the children.

When to Take Survivors Benefits

As with retirement benefits, there are advantages to waiting before you take survivors benefits. A widow or widower can get full benefits by waiting until full retirement age to take them. Taking them early reduces the monthly amount. However, if she or he is taking care of a young child receiving Social Security benefits, there's no penalty for her or him to take benefits early.

If you have children under the age of eighteen, they can take benefits. The Social Security Administration observes, "Under certain circumstances, we can also pay benefits to your stepchildren, grandchildren, stepgrandchildren, or adopted children."

Remarriage

Many times people who've lost a spouse remarry. How does this affect their benefits? Essentially, it depends on how old you are when you remarry. If you're younger than sixty, your survivors benefits will stop. On the other hand, if you're older than sixty (fifty if you're disabled), you can continue to collect benefits based on your former spouse's earnings. After you turn sixty-two, you're eligible to collect spousal benefits based on your new spouse's earnings if that figure would be higher than what you were collecting before.

If your parents are financially dependent on you (that is, if you make up at least half of their financial support) and are at least sixty-two, they may be eligible for Social Security benefits if you precede them in death. If you are divorced and your divorced spouse is at least sixty, she or he can get benefits provided the marriage lasted at least ten years. If she or he is caring for your child and that child is under sixteen or disabled, the widow or widower doesn't have to meet the rule about ten years.

Lump-Sum Death Payment

Social Security will make a one-time lump-sum death benefit payment of $255 to your survivor if one of these conditions holds:

- The survivor was living in the same household as you when the death occurred
- You and your survivor were living apart, but the survivor was receiving benefits on your employee record in the month you died
- The survivor became eligible for benefits upon your death

HOW MUCH?

Just as with normal retirement benefits, the more you made during your lifetime the better off will be your survivors. Your Social Security statement, accessible online through www.ssa.gov/myaccount, will tell you how much your survivors benefits will pay those you leave behind.

The SSA advises that if you're eligible for survivors benefits you should apply right away. This is because in some instances payments will be made from the time you apply and *not* from the time your spouse died. As is the case with any other kinds of Social Security benefits, you can apply online, by phone, or in person. Documents you will need include:

- Proof of death (a death certificate or proof from a funeral home)
- Your Social Security number and that of the deceased
- Your birth certificate
- Your marriage certificate
- Social Security numbers for any dependent children
- Your deceased spouse's W-2 forms or federal self-employment tax return for the most recent year
- Your bank account number and routing number (remember that Social Security payments are deposited directly into your account)

There is a limit on the amount of survivors benefits that can be paid to a family. Total family benefits are limited to between 150–180 percent of the deceased's benefit amount.

Native Americans

Because Native Americans tend to earn less than the rest of the working population (median earnings in 2013 for Native Americans were $34,600, as opposed to $43,000 for the rest of the workforce), they tend to benefit more from Social Security. Social Security is set up in such a way that it pays out more benefits relative to contributions to lower-earning workers than to higher-earning ones. For this reason alone, Native Americans have a strong interest in seeing the system remain healthy and viable.

The Social Security Administration gives these estimates of survivors benefits:

- A widow or widower, at full retirement age or older, generally gets 100 percent of the worker's basic benefit amount;
- A widow or widower, age 60 or older, but under full retirement age, gets about 71–99 percent of the worker's basic benefit amount;
- A widow or widower, any age, with a child younger than age 16, gets 75 percent of the worker's benefit amount; and
- A child gets 75 percent of the worker's benefit amount.

Pensions and Social Security

If your employer has a pension plan (something that's becoming pretty rare these days) and you've already paid Social Security taxes on it, receiving the pension won't have any impact on your Social Security benefits. On the other hand, if you get a pension from somewhere that's not covered by Social Security (for example, the federal government), the SSA may reduce the size of your benefit. We'll discuss this in more detail in the chapter dealing with the Government Pension Offset.

If you haven't reached your full retirement age, it's quite possible that you're still working. This income probably affects the size of the survivors benefit you receive. This is something we'll discuss more in the section about working in retirement. For the moment suffice it to say that there is an upper limit on earnings. If you exceed it while receiving benefits, the size of your benefit will go down. However, this will *only* affect your benefit, not those of other family members.

OTHER BENEFICIARIES

Who Else Can Get Benefits?

The Social Security Administration has to deal with a wide range of classes in administering benefits. These include veterans (both abled and disabled), American citizens living abroad, and qualified citizens of other countries. In this chapter, we'll look at these participants in the Social Security system.

VETERANS

Through the Veterans Administration (VA), if you are a veteran who has been wounded in the course of duty, you may be eligible for veteran benefits. Any number of conditions may cause you to be eligible, including (but not limited to) the following:

- Post-traumatic stress disorder (PTSD)
- Traumatic brain injury
- Post-concussive syndrome
- Military sexual trauma
- Exposure to toxic chemicals (including Agent Orange)
- Orthopedic injuries
- Injuries related to explosions
- Neurological injuries

Receiving veteran benefits does not automatically qualify you to receive Social Security disability benefits. The two sets of benefits have different standards. For instance, you can receive VA disability benefits for partial disability. However, the Social Security system requires that to receive disability benefits from SSA you must be entirely unable to perform your job.

Expedited Benefits

If you became disabled while on active military duty, it's possible to expedite your Social Security benefits, assuming you're eligible for them. Go to www.ssa .gov/people/veterans for more information about how to do this.

MILITARY BENEFITS AND SOCIAL SECURITY

If you served in the U.S. military after 1956, you qualify to receive both military benefits and Social Security benefits (if you served before 1957, you get partial Social Security credit for your service).

You can also be given, in some circumstances, extra credits for your military service. Remember that you need a total of forty credits to become eligible for Social Security benefits, so:

- If you served during the period from 1957 to 1967, the SSA adds extra credits to your earnings record when you apply for Social Security benefits. You are credited with $300 for each quarter in which you received active duty basic pay.
- If you served during the period from 1968 to 2001, the extra credits were automatically added to your record. For every $300

you earned in your military pay, you received another $100 in recorded earnings, up to a maximum of $1,200 per year.

- If you served after 2001, you don't receive any extra credits for your service.

GETTING SOCIAL SECURITY IF YOU'RE LIVING ABROAD

These days, in an effort to beat the cost of living (especially medical care), many American retirees are looking at moving to other countries. Many nations welcome these folks for the money they spend. But retirees often have questions about how living outside the United States will affect their Social Security benefits.

What's Outside the United States?

Just to be clear, by outside the United States, we mean not living in the United States (including Alaska and Hawaii); and not living in any U.S. territory, such as Guam, American Samoa, Puerto Rico, the U.S. Virgin Islands, or the Northern Mariana Islands.

If You're a U.S. Citizen

If you're a citizen of the United States and eligible for Social Security benefits, the SSA will continue to pay those benefits into your bank account.

However, this will not be the case if you live in one of the following countries:

- Cuba
- North Korea
- Azerbaijan
- Belarus
- Georgia
- Kazakhstan

- Kyrgyzstan
- Moldova
- Uzbekistan
- Turkmenistan
- Ukraine
- Vietnam

If you are living in one of those countries and travel to a country where the SSA can send your benefit payments, they'll generally do so. It's also possible in certain circumstances to receive your payment by going to the U.S. embassy in the country. Your local Social Security office can explain these circumstances to you in more detail.

Working in a Foreign Country

If you're working in a foreign country and are younger than your full retirement age, the SSA will not pay benefits for each month you work more than forty-five hours. It doesn't matter how many hours a day you work or how much you earn. The test is if you're working more than forty-five hours a month.

If You're a Citizen of Another Country

If you are an American citizen and become a citizen of another country and are still qualified for American Social Security benefits, you can continue to receive them, assuming you've already filed for them. If you are eligible and haven't yet started to claim them, you can still claim them, provided the country of which you're a citizen is one of the following:

- Austria
- Belgium
- Canada
- Chile
- Czech Republic
- Finland
- France
- Germany
- Greece
- Ireland
- Israel
- Italy
- Japan
- Luxembourg
- Netherlands
- Norway
- Poland
- Portugal
- Slovak Republic
- South Korea
- Spain
- Sweden
- Switzerland
- United Kingdom

REGULAR QUESTIONNAIRES

In order to cut down on fraud and to keep track of its payments, the Social Security Administration sends out regular questionnaires to people who receive Social Security benefits abroad. If you don't return the questionnaire, your benefits will be stopped, which is a pretty good incentive to fill it out and put it in the mail.

BENEFITS FOR CHILDREN

Protecting Young People

In the minds of most people, Social Security is associated with growing old and retiring. Certainly it's true that this is the way most people in the system experience it. But we've already seen that one part of Social Security is designed to help people with disabilities. Still another part aims to assist children.

Roughly 4.3 million children currently receive benefits from Social Security. For many of these, it's because their parent or parents are dead, disabled, or retired. Social Security payments help limit or prevent child poverty.

CHILDREN WHO ARE ELIGIBLE FOR BENEFITS

Of course, not all children can receive benefits. According to the Social Security Administration, one of the following two conditions must exist for a child to be eligible:

1. The child's parent must be disabled or retired and entitled to receive Social Security benefits
2. The child's parent must have died and have worked long enough to be able to start taking Social Security benefits

As well, the child must be unmarried, younger than eighteen (the child can also be eighteen or nineteen and a full-time student still in high school), or eighteen or older and disabled (provided the disability began before age twenty-two). As you can see, while it's not uncommon for a child to qualify for benefits, it's by no means a common occurrence.

Children of Retired Parents

If your child is a dependent (that is, under eighteen, or attending elementary or high school, or disabled—that disability having begun before age twenty-two) and you're retired and taking Social Security benefits, your child is entitled to a benefit that comes to 50 percent of yours. Because of the existence of the family maximum benefit rule, if you have several children who are dependents and can take benefits, each benefit will be smaller than if you only had a single child. Simply put, the more kids you have, the less each kid gets.

Spousal Benefits and Child-in-Care

If you married someone younger than you and you are sixty-two or older and have filed for benefits, your spouse can take benefits before reaching age sixty-two provided that she or he has a child-in-care who is either:

- Under age sixteen
- Mentally disabled and over the age of eighteen but who became disabled before age twenty-two

This can come in handy, especially if you need money right now to take care of your child, and it would be difficult to wait until you and your spouse both reached the claiming age of sixty-two.

DIVORCED AND CHILD-IN-CARE

There's an exception to the rule about spousal benefits and child-in-care. If you're divorced and have a child-in-care, you can't get child-in-care spousal benefits until you turn sixty-two. If this seems unfair, that's because it is. But that's the way the law's written at the moment.

Applying for Benefits

The kinds of documents you'll need to bring with your child when she or he applies for benefits depends on the circumstances. In any case you'll need the child's birth certificate and Social Security number as well as the parent's SSN. If the parent is deceased, you'll need proof of that, either in the form of a death certificate or a note from a funeral home. If the child is disabled, you'll need medical records and contact information for the doctors, clinicians, therapists, and others involved in the child's treatment.

Among the questions the Social Security officials will ask you are:

- Your name and SSN
- The child's name, SSN, and relationship to you (or to the recipient of the Social Security benefits)
- If you're the child's legal or adoptive parent
- If you're the child's legal guardian
- Whether the child has lived with the recipient in the past eighteen months
- If you've ever been convicted of a felony
- Into whose bank account the child's benefits should be paid (be sure to bring your checkbook with your account and routing numbers)

Benefits end when the child turns eighteen. At that point, the SSA presumes that your son or daughter can start earning a living and accumulating her or his own credits toward Social Security.

Care of a Child

According to the SSA:

- If you're receiving benefits because you have a child in your care, the date your benefits stop can be different than the child's.
- If the child isn't disabled, your benefits will end when he or she turns 16.
- If the child is disabled, your benefits can continue if you exercise parental control and responsibility for a mentally disabled child. Your benefits can also continue if you perform personal services for a child who's physically disabled.

You may remember from an earlier chapter that there's a limit to how much Social Security will pay to any one family. The family maximum payment is generally 150–180 percent of the parent's full benefit.

In Your Care

A child is in your care, in the view of the SSA, if she or he spends at least a day per month with you. This is particularly important if you and your spouse are divorced and have joint custody of the child.

CHILDREN OF DIVORCED PARENTS

The whole issue of benefits to children and their parents becomes much more complicated when the parents divorce. We talked a little bit about this when we were discussing spousal benefits, but it's time to come back to it again.

The basic rule, you may recall, is that if your marriage lasted longer than ten years, your ex can collect spousal benefits based on your earnings record (assuming it's higher than his or hers) or vice versa.

When Is Ten Years Not Ten Years?

The Social Security rules get very pedantic when it comes to the ten-year rule about divorced spousal benefits. It's not just a total of ten years that you have to be married but ten *consecutive* years. For instance, if John and Mary were married from 2000 to 2010 and then divorced, Mary can collect spousal benefits based on John's earnings. But if they were married in 2000, divorced in 2006, remarried the following year, and divorced in 2015, Mary's out of luck. They were, in fact, married for a total of fourteen years, but the years weren't consecutive. From the SSA's viewpoint it doesn't count, and so Mary will have to base her benefits on her own earnings record.

TAXES ON SOCIAL SECURITY BENEFITS

Giving the Government What's Theirs

Wait a minute, I can hear you saying. I already paid taxes—the FICA payroll tax—just to get my Social Security benefit in the first place. Do you mean the federal government's going to tax me *again*? I thought I got past all that when I retired.

Well, yes and no. It's true that some portion of people receiving Social Security have to pay taxes on their benefits. However, this tax is pretty much assessed on people at the upper end of the income scale—presumably people who can afford it.

Currently, about 40 percent of beneficiaries pay taxes on their benefits. Even if you count yourself among the lucky 60 percent who don't pay these taxes, you should still understand how taxes are figured on benefits so you don't have any nasty surprises come April 15.

FIGURING YOUR INCOME

The key to finding out if you owe taxes on your benefits is understanding how to calculate your income. This is different when you're on Social Security than when you had a full-time job.

To calculate your income:

1. Take half of your total Social Security benefits amount
2. Take all other income, including interest on savings, any money you earned from capital gains, and so forth

3. Add the two numbers together

This final tally is what the Social Security Administration regards as your income. Actually, they refer to it as your "provisional income."

If you file for benefits as a single person and your annual provisional income falls below $25,000, you don't owe taxes on your benefits. If your provisional income is more than $25,000 and less than $34,000, you will owe taxes on 50 percent of your benefits. If your provisional income is above $34,000, you'll owe taxes on 85 percent of your benefits.

If you file as a married couple, the limits are higher: The lower limit is $32,000, and the upper limit is $44,000. (Please note that these numbers are as of 2016; like most other Social Security numbers, they're subject to change by congressional action.)

EXAMPLES OF SOCIAL SECURITY BENEFITS TAX

How does this work in practice?

Let's imagine you are a single person and have waited until your full retirement age of sixty-seven to claim your benefit. Your monthly benefit works out to $2,007. Are you going to have to pay taxes?

Case A

If you don't have any other income than Social Security, your provisional incomes amounts to $12,042 ($2,007 × 12 months = $24,084 ÷ 2 = $12,042). This is below the limit of $25,000 for a single individual, so your benefits will be tax-free.

Case B

Now let's suppose that in addition to your benefits, you have several other sources of income. You take annual distributions from an IRA and your 401(k) account that add up to $16,000; and you do freelance work for your old employer, which generates an additional $5,000 per year. Now your provisional income amounts to $33,042 ($12,042 + $16,000 + $5,000). Your provisional income is more than $25,000 but less than $34,000—which, remember, is the upper limit for individuals. You'll owe taxes on 50 percent of your benefits.

Case C

What about filing as a married couple? Well, say that you and your husband have both reached your full retirement ages and claimed benefits. Yours is $2,007, and his is $1,836. To get your provisional income, assuming you have no other sources of income, add the two benefits together, multiply by twelve, and divide by two. Your provisional income is $23,058. You're below the $32,000 that's the lower limit for married couples, so you're in luck. No tax is due on your benefits. However, if you were to have any other sources of income, you might exceed the limit, and so a portion of your benefits would be taxed.

YOUR TAX RATE

Note that the amount of money you pay in taxes on your benefits (assuming you're taxed on them) is determined by your marginal tax rate. The following table indicates what these rates are.

MARGINAL TAX RATE	SINGLE FILER INCOME	MARRIED, FILING JOINTLY INCOME
10%	Up to $9,275	Up to $18,550
15%	$9,275 to $37,650	$18,550 to $75,300
25%	$37,650 to $91,150	$75,300 to $151,900
28%	$91,150 to $190,150	$151,900 to $231,450
33%	$190,150 to $413,350	$231,450 to $413,350
35%	$413,350 to $415,050	$413,350 to $466,950
39.6%	$415,050+	$466,950+

If you must pay taxes on your benefits, you may find it advisable to use the services of a tax professional to determine precisely how much you owe Uncle Sam.

WORKING IN RETIREMENT

The Pluses and Minuses of More Income

For many people, retirement means complete relaxation. You get up in the morning when you want, do things at your own pace, potter around the house and the yard, and generally relax. This is the life you've been looking forward to all those years when you were working away at your job.

For others, though, retirement just means slowing the pace of work, not giving it up altogether. There's nothing wrong with either of these retirement schemes; it's just a matter of which suits you better.

THE BENEFITS OF WORKING

As we'll discuss shortly, there are excellent reasons to continue in your full-time job until age seventy. Such a course increases the size of your benefit to its maximum amount. Conversely, there are compelling reasons to avoid, if at all possible, taking your benefits before you reach your full retirement age. If you do this, you will reduce, permanently, the size of the benefit Social Security pays you each month. Naturally, for some people this isn't an option. There are all kinds of reasons why you might claim your benefits when you reach the age of sixty-two, the earliest point at which you can take them. But it's generally better to wait (although not always, as we'll see in a while).

There are other significant benefits to continuing to work as long as possible or until age seventy. They include:

- **Benefits packages.** Most employers offer a significant benefits package to their employees, which may include health insurance, life insurance, vision coverage, and other perks.
- **Savings plans.** Many companies offer their employees an opportunity to enroll in 401(k) plans, which are an excellent means of saving for retirement. In some, though not all, cases, employers will match a percentage of employee contributions to the plan.
- **A steady paycheck.** One of the biggest benefits of working, of course, is the prospect of a weekly or biweekly check.

Of course, there are disadvantages of working late in life as well.

- Despite government mandates against it, age discrimination exists in the workplace. As you grow older, you may find it harder to get promotions or to move into different positions at work. You may watch as younger employees with less experience are promoted above you. And, of course, there is the danger of finding your position eliminated because your boss doesn't want to keep someone at your salary level on the payroll.
- If you're let go, you'll probably find it harder to get a new job. Most employers want to hire people who will stay with the company a long time, not someone who quite clearly is going to retire in a few years.
- Physically, continuing to work into your late sixties may be challenging. Despite our best efforts to stay in shape, aging affects our bodies. We find it harder to perform some of the tasks at work that were easy to do when we were younger. Physical ailments

may start to become a real problem: arthritis, and deteriorating vision and hearing, for example. And, chances are, we won't be able to maintain the energy levels we once had ten or fifteen years previously.

All of these are issues to consider when you're deciding when to stop working and start collecting your Social Security benefits. But instead of just riding off into the sunset, let's talk about working *while* taking benefits.

ANNUAL EARNINGS LIMIT

The bad news is that Social Security places a limit on how much you can earn while taking benefits. The good news is that this limit ends once you reach your full retirement age.

How does the limit work?

As of 2016, the annual earnings limit if you're under your full retirement age is $15,720. For every $2 you earn above that limit, the SSA deducts $1 from your benefit.

For the year you reach your full retirement age, the limit goes up to $41,880 (this number is as of 2016 and is subject to change). In that year, the SSA deducts $1 for every $3 you earn above this limit.

Defining Earnings

When the Social Security Administration looks at your earnings, they count wages, bonuses, vacation pay, and commissions. They do *not* count pensions, annuities, investment income, or veteran benefits.

Finally, when you pass your full retirement age, the limit goes away entirely, and your benefits are not affected by your earnings. Moreover, Social Security then recalculates your benefit to give you credit for any years in which you didn't receive benefits because of your earnings.

How Benefits Are Withheld

Generally, if your earnings put you over the limit, the SSA will hold back a certain number of months of benefits until the withholding amount that they calculated is met. However, you can request that instead they prorate the withholding, meaning that a small amount is held back from each monthly benefit.

The practical upshot of this system is that if you continue to work while taking benefits, and if you're younger than your full retirement age, your benefits will increase, possibly by a substantial amount, once you've passed your FRA. However—and this is a very big however—if you take your benefits after age sixty-two but before your full retirement age, the amount of your benefits will be permanently reduced and you will have no way of increasing them.

How does this work in practice?

Case A

Roger has turned sixty-two and qualifies for a monthly benefit of $1,500 if he begins his benefits now. If he waits until his full retirement age, which in his case is sixty-six, his benefit will rise to $2,000. Roger's employer asks him to stay on as a part-time employee at an annual salary of $25,000.

If Roger takes his Social Security benefits now, his annual income will be $43,000 ($1,500 × 12 months = $18,000 + $25,000 = $43,000). Since this is $27,280 above the $15,720 limit ($43,000

– $15,720 = $27,280) for earnings prior to full retirement age, some of Roger's benefits will be deducted—$1 for every $2 he's above the limit. This means Roger will lose $13,640 in benefits ($27,280 ÷ 2), and his annual Social Security benefits will only amount to $4,360, or $363.00 per month. As the math shows, it doesn't make any sense for him to take benefits now; it's better for him to keep working—if possible, full-time with a full-time salary.

Case B

As it so happens, Roger decides to take early benefits anyway. It's now the year in which Roger will turn sixty-six, his full retirement age. His birthday is in December. The annual earnings limit has now risen to $41,880. Roger's salary of $43,000 is still above the limit, but not by very much. He's over by $1,120 ($43,000 – $41,880 = $1,120). Since the SSA withholds $1 for every $3 he's over the limit, the total withheld from his benefits will be $373.33 ($1,120 ÷ 3). Remember, his benefit checks are $363.00 per month. Therefore the SSA will withhold the first three benefit checks of the year (for a total of $339.99) and pay the fourth check at $79.99 to complete the amount withheld. The checks will go back to $113.33 per month for the rest of the year until December when they will rise to Roger's full benefit amount of $1,500.

It would have been a better idea for Roger not to take benefits at all until he turned his full retirement age (in which case he'd now be getting $2,000 a month). However, there may be circumstances in which people feel compelled to start their benefits early. We'll look at some of these circumstances shortly.

TAKING BENEFITS EARLY

Don't Do It Unless . . .

As mentioned several times in this book, there are three times at which to claim your benefits:

1. Between age sixty-two and your full retirement age (FRA)
2. At your full retirement age
3. Between your full retirement age and age seventy

We've also suggested a number of times that in general it's a bad idea to take your benefits early. The reason is that if you wait, the size of your benefit will grow. If you start collecting benefits at age sixty-two, you could be cheating yourself out of a substantial amount of money. That said, an article in news magazine *U.S. News & World Report* commented that age sixty-two continues to be the most popular age at which to take benefits:

> Some 45 percent of men born in 1943 and 1944 signed up for retirement benefits at age 62, down from 50 percent of people born between 1938 and 1942, and a peak of 57 percent of men born between 1930 and 1934, according to a 2013 Urban Institute analysis of U.S. Census Bureau data. The share of women claiming Social Security benefits at age 62 has also declined over the past decade, but women continue to be more likely to claim early than men. Half of women born in 1943 or 1944 claimed at age 62, compared with 60 percent of those born between 1935 and 1937.

A CASE HISTORY

For example, let's take Wilson, who was born in 1954. He's single, and based on his family history and his personal habits—he's a non-smoker, a moderate drinker, and exercises during the week and on weekends—his life expectancy is somewhere around eight-five.

Wilson's always had a dream of starting a small business; he'd like to open a used bookstore to serve the small town in which he lives and the surrounding communities. He intends to use a good chunk of his savings to launch the business, but he sees his Social Security benefit as providing enough for his everyday expenses. He has some investments that he's counting on to produce good returns. And, of course, once the bookstore starts to turn a profit he'll have that income as well.

With this in mind, Wilson examines his Social Security statement and finds that his monthly benefit will be $1,429 a month or $17,148 a year. That seems a bit low, but Wilson figures that with some penny pinching, he can get along. He files for benefits on his sixty-second birthday and gets down to starting to put his dream in action: finding storefront space, acquiring stock, and so on.

As it happens, a number of things go wrong: Wilson finds that rental space for the store is substantially more than he estimated. Moreover, marketing his business takes a great deal of his time and energy, and to top it off, the economy slows down: his investments stagnate and his business lags. Worry and overwork combine to necessitate a hospital stay that runs up more than $100,000 in medical bills. Increasingly reliant on his Social Security benefit, he realizes it's inadequate to cover his expenses, and he begins the painfully slow process of job searching. His dream of a happy and productive retirement turns out to be just that: a dream.

The Virtue of Patience

What would have happened if Wilson had waited four more years until reaching his full retirement age? His benefit would have been $2,006 a month, or $24,072 a year, $6,924 more per year than his current benefit.

Assuming that Wilson lives to his estimated age of eighty-five, with his current benefit, he'll accumulate $394,404 over the rest of his life. This sounds like a lot of money, but if he had waited until reaching his full retirement age, that sum would have become $457,368.

But there's a third alternative. Wilson could wait until he turns seventy to take his benefits. This will mean fewer years of retirement, of course, but the reward can be financial security.

If Wilson waits until he turns seventy to claim Social Security benefits, his monthly benefit will amount to $2,787 a month or $33,444 a year. Assuming he lives to age eighty-five, he'll collect a total of $501,660. By waiting until age seventy, Wilson will increase his payout from Social Security by more than $100,000.

Should You Make Investments?

One argument for taking early benefits is that you can invest all or a portion of the money and reap excellent returns. This assumes two things: first that you have another source of income that you can live on while your money is invested (at least until those investments start to pay dividends), and second that you know how to invest wisely. Both those assumptions are questionable. Many people make poor investing decisions, and the markets can turn quickly (remember the 2008 market crash, anyone?). Leaving your money in the Social Security system is a far safer way of planning for the future.

THE ISSUE OF LIFE EXPECTANCY

The key in all this, you'll notice, is the issue of how long you're likely to live. The life expectancy table we showed in the chapter Your Full Retirement Age can help you estimate this, but there are some other things you should take into consideration.

- **What's your family history?** If a lot of your family members have lived to a ripe old age, there's a pretty good chance that genetics are going to work in your favor. It pays to investigate your family history and try to get an average of the lifespans of the men and women who are part of it.
- **Do you smoke?** A 2013 study printed in the *New England Journal of Medicine* estimated that smoking takes at least ten years off your life. On the other hand, the study found, if you give up smoking before age forty, you reduce the risk to your life by up to 90 percent.
- **Do you drink?** Sure, most of us probably like to kick back with a beer or a glass of wine occasionally. But if you're a habitual drinker (meaning you drink several alcoholic beverages every day), a 2013 study in the *American Journal of Public Health* suggests you may be shortening your life expectancy by as much as two decades.
- **Do you have a high-risk or high-stress job?** Some stress is inevitable with any job. But if you're feeling under constant stress, the hormones your body is producing will damage important tissue, knocking years off your life.
- **Do you have a healthy diet and exercise regularly?** By regularly we mean at least thirty minutes a day. Walking or running

counts, as well as any workout you do at the gym. A healthy diet should include all the food groups and avoid fatty and deep-fried foods. You don't have to go all granola; just use common sense.

Consider all of these factors when you're deciding whether to take your Social Security benefits early.

WHEN—IF EVER—SHOULD YOU TAKE EARLY BENEFITS?

Despite the fact that the overwhelming majority of financial experts urge you to hold off taking benefits until you reach your full retirement age (and, if possible, until you reach age seventy), there are some exceptions to taking them earlier.

It's Okay to Take Early Benefits?

In keeping with its often-contrarian character, the financial advisory service the Motley Fool writes in a January 2016 column that it makes sense to take benefits early. They quote the U.S. Government Accountability Office to this effect: "The Social Security benefit formula adjusts monthly payments so that someone living to average life expectancy should receive about the same amount of benefits over their lifetime regardless of which age they claim." Therefore, write the folks at the Fool, "If you can wait to take Social Security benefits, that's great. Go ahead and do so. But if you can't or don't want to, then there's no reason to second-guess your decision to take them early."

Do You Need the Money Now?

Americans have very bad savings habits. A survey in 2014, taken in conjunction with the annual America Saves Week, found that 51 percent of Americans had a specific savings goal, and only 35 percent felt they were making good progress in meeting that goal. The upshot is that many people reach the age at which they want to retire and rely on Social Security, even a reduced benefit, to pay the bills. This is particularly true for people who are finding it increasingly difficult to stay on the job.

Is Your Life Expectancy Low?

If, after looking at charts and figures, you conclude that you're unlikely to live much beyond seventy, it doesn't make much sense to wait until seventy to take your benefits. Of course, you might wait until reaching your full retirement age, but you may wish to have as long a retirement as possible. In that case, claiming early benefits is probably the right thing to do.

Finally, it's worth pointing out that sixty-two is by far the most popular age at which to claim benefits. So even though it usually makes more financial sense to wait, the majority of retirees want their money as soon as possible.

CLAIMING BENEFITS LATER

Increasing the Size of Your Benefit

It's a sad truth that many elderly people slip into poverty as they grow older. One of the most important reasons is rising medical costs and the need for increasingly expensive procedures designed to keep them alive. Another factor is that people underestimate how long they'll live, and they outlive their savings. This situation is particularly difficult for people who took early Social Security benefits, thus permanently reducing the size of those benefits. They often discover that it is difficult to subsist on a small sum from Social Security with no other streams of income.

The two best ways to avoid falling into this trap are, first, to increase your savings, which will provide another source of retirement income, and, second, to increase the size of your benefits. To do either or both of these may involve some sacrifice now. You're putting money away for the future, not spending it now on stuff you want. You will have to decide that a secure future is worth a frugal present, and then take steps to make that future a reality.

TAKING THE CREDIT

The difference in taking your benefits at full retirement age and taking them at age seventy may be striking. For each year you work past your full retirement age, the government gives you a credit worth 8 percent of your benefit. In other words, if your retirement age is sixty-seven and you work three years past it to age seventy, your benefit grows by 24 percent.

BREAKING EVEN

One of the most common tools to determine whether or not you should take benefits early or wait it out is called a break-even analysis.

Expecting Beyond Expectancy

As said earlier, a lot of factors go into determining life expectancy. One of these factors has to do with how the life expectancy tables themselves are calculated. The basic calculation of life expectancy averages a cross-sample of males and females. This includes people who die when they're very young as well as very old. If you're a man, your expected lifespan is seventy-five. But if you live to be sixty-two, your life expectancy increases to eighty-two. For women who live to sixty-two, life expectancy increases from eighty-one to eighty-five.

Essentially, a break-even analysis tells you how long you need to take benefits to receive the monetary value you'd get if you took them earlier or later. Keep in mind the way benefits work: If you claim them before reaching your full retirement age, you get more checks, but they're smaller. If you claim at or after your full retirement age, there are fewer checks, but they're bigger.

Let's look at an example. Mark, who has just turned sixty-two, decides to claim his benefit of $750 per month. Linda, who is the same age, determines that she'll wait until her full retirement age of sixty-six, at which point her benefit will be $1,000. Neal, also turning sixty-two, decides to wait to claim until he turns seventy, when he'll claim $1,320 per month. The following table shows the cumulative amount of money they've received from Social Security.

BREAK-EVEN ANALYSIS FOR MARK, LINDA, AND NEAL (ANNUAL BENEFITS)			
Age	Mark	Linda	Neal
62	$9,000	$0	$0
63	$18,000	$0	$0
64	$27,000	$0	$0
65	$36,000	$0	$0
66	$45,000	$12,000	$0
67	$54,000	$24,000	$0
68	$63,000	$36,000	$0
69	$72,000	$48,000	$0
70	$81,000	$60,000	$15,840
71	$90,000	$72,000	$31,680
72	$99,000	$84,000	$47,520
73	$108,000	$96,000	$63,360
74	$117,000	$108,000	$79,200
75	$126,000	$120,000	$95,040
76	$135,000	$132,000	$110,880
77	$144,000	$144,000	$126,720
78	$153,000	$156,000	$142,560
79	$162,000	$168,000	$158,400
80	$171,000	$180,000	$174,240
81	$180,000	$192,000	$190,080
82	$189,000	$204,000	$205,920

Notice that even though Mark got money in years when Linda and Neal didn't, their totals caught up to his and surpassed it. In Neal's case, this happened quite quickly—by age eighty, after he'd been taking benefits for ten years. So Neal's and Mark's break-even point is eighty, while Linda's and Mark's is seventy-seven. Neal's and

Linda's is eighty-two. Another way of putting this is that for Mark to justify his decision to collect benefits before waiting until his retirement age, he'll have to live until at least age seventy-seven. Linda, to justify her decision not to wait until age seventy as Neal did, will have to live to age eighty-two.

"Social Security is based on a principle. It's based on the principle that you care about other people. You care whether the widow across town, a disabled widow, is going to be able to have food to eat."

—Noam Chomsky, American linguist

However, it's worth noting that the Social Security Administration no longer uses break-even analyses when it advises people on benefits. The reason is that the analysis leaves out too much: What about the health, habits, and family histories of each individual? What about their stress levels? What about the physical environments in which they work? (Someone who works in a building that contains asbestos fibers isn't likely to have a long life expectancy, no matter what the family history!)

TAKING YOUR BENEFITS LATE

We come back to the point made earlier. Unless there's a specific reason to do so, it's best *not* to take your benefits earlier than your full retirement age. In fact, it's generally best to wait until age seventy before taking them.

Consider the preceding example that compares Mark, Linda, and Neal. By the time they reach age eighty-five, Mark's total has reached $216,000, Linda's $240,000, and Neal's has totaled a whopping $253,440. That's more than $37,000 more than Mark. And that amount increases exponentially as the years advance. By age ninety, Mark's accumulated Social Security benefits amount to $261,000 but Neal by that time has benefits of $332,640. Now he's more than $71,600 ahead of Mark.

Social Security in Australia

The system of retirement benefits down under dates to 1992 and is called a Superannuation Guarantee. Unlike most social insurance systems, employees don't have to contribute to the fund, although they are encouraged to do so. Employers' contributions amount to 9.5 percent (between 2021 and 2025, this percentage will gradually grow to 12 percent). Funds are divided into three types:

- Preserved benefits. These cannot be accessed by the employee until she or he turns fifty-five if born before July 1960, rising to sixty if born after June 1964.
- Restricted non-preserved benefits. These can be accessed under specific circumstances.
- Unrestricted non-preserved benefits. These can be accessed upon the worker's request, although certain conditions still apply.

All of this assumes—and this can't be stressed enough—that you've evaluated your probable life expectancy and all the factors that go into it. If there is a reasonable probability of you living until your full retirement age and beyond, it makes eminent sense to delay taking benefits and enjoy the larger sums when they start.

IF YOU'RE SELF-EMPLOYED

The Challenge of Working for Yourself

As of 2015, approximately 15 million Americans were self-employed, about 10.1 percent of the working population. This is a very significant number of people. For many, working for themselves is a lifelong dream—to be free of bosses, office routines, irritating coworkers ... The thought of working out of your home and deciding your own hours and work goals is enormously attractive to many people.

However, Social Security can present concerns, and even shocks, to self-employed people. The fact is that although you work for yourself, you haven't opted out of U.S. government-administered systems. And that means you will pay taxes.

SELF-EMPLOYMENT AND TAXES

In some ways, your tax situation as a self-employed person is far more complicated than if you worked for a company. For one thing, the company arranges for your taxes to be automatically deducted from your paycheck every fortnight (or however often you're paid). However, as your own boss you are now responsible for making sure that your taxes are paid—including the payroll taxes that fund Social Security and Medicare. If you earn more than $400 a year, you must file tax Schedule SE (in addition to other forms).

If you work for an employer, matters regarding the Social Security tax are pretty simple. You pay 6.2 percent, and your employer pays 6.2 percent for Social Security; and both you and your employer pay the 1.45 percent tax to fund Medicare. However, if you're self-employed, the government assumes that you are *both* employer and employed. You have to pay both halves of the tax: 12.4 percent for Social Security and 2.9 percent for Medicare. That suddenly doubled tax burden can come as a shock—particularly in the early days of your self-employed career when your income isn't all that large and you're scrambling to find new gigs.

Deductions

The good news is that you're allowed to take some deductions you wouldn't be permitted if you worked for someone else. For example:

- Your net earnings are reduced by half the amount of Social Security tax that you paid.
- When filling out Form 1040, you can deduct half your Social Security tax. However, this deduction isn't itemized; you take it from your gross income when figuring your adjusted gross income.

Wages and Self-Employment Earnings

If you have both wages paid by an employer and self-employment earnings, and if they total more than $118,500, you must pay taxes on the wages first. For example, if Roger earns $75,000 from his job and in addition makes $50,000 in freelance work from his self-employment business, his employer will withhold taxes on his wages. Roger will pay Social Security and Medicare on $43,500 ($118,500 – $43,500 = $75,000) and will pay Medicare on the remaining $6,500 ($125,000 – $6,500 = $118,500).

NET EARNINGS

For purposes of figuring your net earnings, Social Security counts your gross earnings minus allowable business deductions and depreciation. When figuring your net earnings from your business, you should *not* include:

- Dividends from stocks or interest on bonds (unless your business involves selling stocks and securities, in which case the income you received from those sales does count toward net earnings)
- Interest derived from loans (unless, of course, you're a professional lender)
- Rents from real estate (unless you're a real-estate dealer)
- Income from a limited partnership

If You Earn Less Than $400

If you're in the early stages of your self-employment, it is possible that your net earnings will fall below $400. However, you can still count this for Social Security purposes. Here's how the SSA explains it:

- If your gross income from farm self-employment was not more than $7,560, or your net farm profits were less than $5,457, you may report the smaller of two-thirds of gross farm income (not less than 0) or $5,040; or
- If your net income from non-farm self-employment is less than $5,457 and also less than 72.189% of your gross non-farm income, and you had net earnings from self-employment of at least $400 in 2 of the prior 3 years.

- You can use both the farm and non-farm methods of reporting, and can report less than your total actual net earnings from farm and non-farm self-employment, but you can't report less than your actual net earnings from non-farm self-employment alone. If you use both methods to figure net earnings, you can't report more than $5,040.

You're only allowed to use this optional method five times in your life *except* if you're a farmer. If you are, you can use this method every year, and you don't have to have earned at least $400 the previous year.

You can find additional information about the optional method of reporting in the IRS's *Tax Guide for Small Business*, located online at www.irs.gov/pub/irs-pdf/p334.pdf.

WHICH TAX FORMS TO FILL OUT

In any year in which your business earns $400 or more in net earnings, you need to fill out the following IRS forms:

- Form 1040
- Schedule C

DEEMED FILING

Issues with Suspending Benefits

The passage of the Bipartisan Budget Act in 2015 had some significant effects on the way people could claim their Social Security benefits. One of these was in the area called "deemed filing."

The simplest explanation of deemed filing is that when you file for either your retirement benefits or your spousal benefits, you are "deemed" by the Social Security Administration to have filed for all the benefits to which you're entitled. In other words, the SSA treats an application for one set of benefits as an application for *both* retirement and spousal benefits, and it pays you the larger of the two.

WHAT CHANGED?

Prior to the act's passing, the deemed rule only applied if you took benefits before your full retirement age. What Congress did through the act was to extend this to full retirement age and beyond.

"Deemed filing doesn't apply to widows and widowers. You can still file for only your own or only the widow(er)'s benefits, then switch to the other later. It's a great planning opportunity if you've lost a spouse or even an ex-spouse."

—Andy Landis, author of *Social Security: The Inside Story*

This rule change applies to you if you turned sixty-two *after* January 1, 2016. If you were sixty-two prior to this date, deeming only applies if you're taking benefits before reaching your full retirement age but not after.

It should be noted that this rule applies only to retirement benefits, not other kinds of benefits (disability, widow/widower, etc.). The exception is divorced spouses, where the new law does apply.

Social Security in France

Like most things French, Social Security there is complicated. Some form of it has been in place since 1910. It is a voluntary system, insuring retirement benefits for those who pay a tax of 6.65 percent. The employer pays 8.3 percent. To qualify you must be at least sixty years old. There are also parallel schemes for survivors benefits, disability, and maternity.

An Example

Let's see how this works in practice.

Janice and William are married. William has reached his full retirement age of sixty-seven, while Janice is only sixty-two. William files for his full benefits of $2,360 a month, and Janice files for her spousal benefits, which she calculates at $1,003, with the intent to take her own benefits later. When her first check arrives, though, she's startled to see that it's for a higher amount: $1,625. Puzzled, she contacts the SSA and is informed that the agency has deemed that even though she only filed for her spousal benefit, in fact she filed for both benefits. Her regular retirement benefit is $1,625, which is obviously more than $1,003, and therefore the SSA is sending out her own retirement benefits and not spousal benefits.

Which would be okay except that now Janice's benefit is permanently stuck at this pre-full retirement level (for age sixty-two). Even if she waits until age seventy, the amount of her benefit isn't going to go up.

Particularly with the new changes in Social Security, this is yet another reason to think long and hard before claiming benefits early. A mistake such as Janice's can cost you thousands and thousands of dollars in the long run.

FILE AND SUSPEND

Another related filing strategy that Congress took away is called file and suspend. We've talked about this earlier, but it bears repeating. The strategy, the unintended result of a number of years of incremental changes to the Social Security system, had become increasingly popular as a loophole through which couples could maximize their benefits. Perhaps it shouldn't have come as a surprise that the government, looking to shore up the system, closed that particular loophole.

Here's how it worked. In 2000, changes to the law made it possible for workers to file for benefits and then suspend them. The suspended benefits would continue to gain delayed retirement credits (DRCs), meaning that when they were resumed, they'd be at a higher level. However, other benefits such as spouse and family benefits weren't suspended.

The practical upshot was that a worker could file and then immediately suspend his benefits, which would accumulate DRCs until such time as he took them. His spouse could file for spousal benefits

Your Social Security card is one of the most important documents you own. It marks your entry into the government-run retirement system, paid for by deductions from employee paychecks.

President Franklin Roosevelt signed the Social Security Act into law in 1935 in response to the Great Depression. He intended the system to keep older people from falling into poverty.

Opposite page: Social Security funds are invested in U.S. Treasury Bonds, one of the safest investments there is since the bonds are backed by the full good faith of the government.

To apply for a Social Security card for you or your child, you'll need various specified forms of identification, which can include a driver's license and a passport.

This page: The question of when to start taking your benefits is key to a successful retirement. Most financial experts advise delaying the start of benefits as long as possible.

Photo Credits: © iStockphoto.com/larryhw; Robert Mizerek/123RF; zimmytws/123RF

This page: Taking disabilities can present challenges, since the Social Security Administration requires proof that you can't do your job or any related job making use of your skills.

Opposite page: The amount of your monthly benefits increases over time provided you delay taking Social Security until you at least reach your full retirement age.

Financial planners can be an enormous help in strategizing about your retirement, but you must find one who is the right fit for you and who understands clearly what kind of retirement you want.

Photo Credits: © Brian Jackson/123RF; iStockphoto.com/Laura Young; racorn/123RF

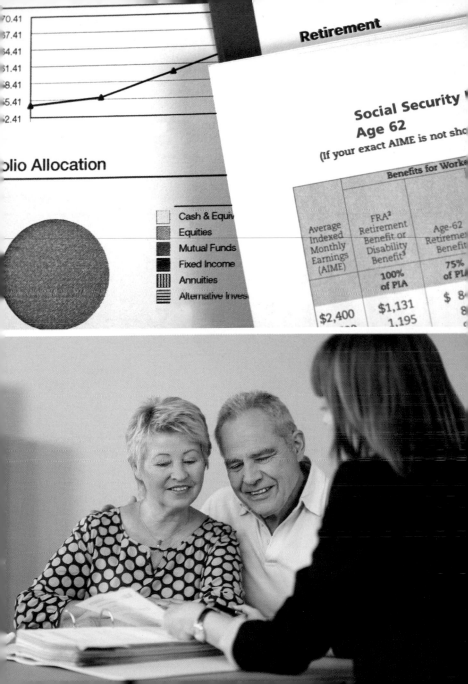

This page: Social Security was never intended as the sole source of retirement income. Rather, it should be part of a larger plan involving multiple income streams.

Opposite page: With good planning, you and your loved ones can live a long, financially healthy retirement. Social Security can be an essential part of that if you learn how to make the most of it.

Photo Credits: © iqoncept/123RF; dmbaker/123RF

Your golden years can be lived out in many settings, provided you plan and make the necessary adjustments to your lifestyle. Learning about Social Security early is important to achieving that goal.

and avoid taking her own benefit, leaving it to grow until she reached her full retirement age (or seventy, if she could delay that long).

The Bipartisan Budget Act in 2015 changed this situation by mandating that after April 16, 2016, suspending one benefit will have the effect of suspending *all* benefits. This change prevents the worker's wife or husband from claiming spousal benefits.

Another thing the Bipartisan Budget Act did was to eliminate what's known as a restricted application. A restricted application allowed a spouse to file for *only* spousal benefits. This scheme was essentially the answer to the deeming issue; without a restricted application the person applying for spousal benefits would be deemed by the SSA to have applied for all her or his benefits and would have to take whichever benefit was larger: spousal or normal retirement benefits.

Phase-Out Time

Unlike the file and suspend strategy, which went away in April 2016, the restricted application rule will take some time to disappear. If you were born in 1953 or earlier, you can still file a restricted application. If you were born after that, the deeming rule applies to any applications you make for benefits.

An August 2009 study for the Center for Retirement Research indicated that "[t]he potential cost of allowing couples the option of 'Claim and Suspend' is about $0.5 billion a year." The study further commented (somewhat ironically, given Congress's actions in 2015) that of the various claiming strategies the authors studied, file and suspend "appears to have the clearest policy rationale as it provides an incentive for individuals to work longer."

INTEREST-FREE LOAN?
NOT ANY MORE

Prior to 2010, it was possible for employees to claim benefits at sixty-two and then, upon reaching full retirement age, repay all the benefits they'd received and begin taking benefits at the higher number dictated by their FRA. In effect, they got an interest-free loan while their benefits continued to build up delayed retirement credits.

In December 2010 the Social Security Administration announced a change to these rules, which the Center for Retirement Research had estimated could cost the system up to $8.7 billion a year. Instead, beneficiaries are only allowed to pay back the amount of their benefits in the first twelve months after they take them. Furthermore, beneficiaries are only allowed to engage in this payback once in their lifetimes.

WINDFALL ELIMINATION PROVISION

Working for Two Different Kinds of Employers

So far we've been largely talking about situations in which you've worked your entire career in jobs under which you qualified for Social Security benefits. But of course, that's sometimes not the case. If you worked for both an employer who withheld Social Security payroll taxes and one who didn't (for example, the federal government), your benefits may be affected by something called the Windfall Elimination Provision.

WHAT IS IT?

The Windfall Elimination Provision grew out of a simple fact about Social Security: The system is designed to benefit lower-income people. To understand why this is the case, we need to look a bit more closely at how the Social Security Administration calculates your benefits.

The SSA starts by figuring out your thirty-five top earning years. As has been pointed out, if you only worked thirty years, the remaining five years will be counted as zeros (no income). Then the SSA adds up all your earnings for your top-earning thirty-five years, any zeros included.

That total earnings number is divided by 420 months (which is thirty-five years). This gives your average monthly earning during those thirty-five years (also known as average indexed monthly earnings or AIME).

Now the SSA does some calculations with the AIME. They multiply the first $856 by 90 percent. Then they multiply the amount from $856 through $5,157 by 32 percent. (This assumes, of course, that your AIME got that high.) Finally, whatever is left above $5,157 they multiply by 15 percent. They add these three sums together, and the result is your monthly benefit if you retire at your full retirement age.

An Example

Let's see how this works. We'll take Ron, whose full retirement age is sixty-seven. SSA looks at his highest-earning thirty-five years. Because of bouts of unemployment and schooling, Ron didn't work for seven of those years, so for SSA purposes they count as zero earnings. Nonetheless, the total of these years is a whopping $3,264,874.

Now the SSA divides this number by 420. This means Ron's AIME is $7,773.51. We'll round it down to the nearest dollar, just as the SSA does. The first $856 of this is multiplied by 90 percent, giving us $770, rounded to the nearest dollar. Then they take $4,301 (the amount of AIME between $5,157 and $856) and multiply it by 32 percent. That gives $1,376. Finally, they take $2,616 (the amount between $7,773 and $4,301) and multiply it by 15 percent, which gives us $392. Add those three numbers together, and we get $2,538. Thus, Ron's monthly benefit will be $2,538 if he retires and starts taking his benefits at his full retirement age.

For comparison purposes, let's look at Marcie, whose full retirement age is also sixty-seven. Her AIME is less than Ron's; it's $4,224. Ninety percent of the first $856 of this is $770. Then the SSA takes $3,454 (the amount of Marcie's AIME remaining) and multiplies it by 32 percent, giving us $1,105. The SSA adds the $770 to the $1,105, and determines Marcie's monthly benefit to be $1,875 when she reaches her FRA.

SOCIAL SECURITY BENEFITS LOW-INCOME WORKERS

As the Center on Budget and Policy Priorities remarks:

> Social Security benefits are progressive: they represent a higher proportion of a worker's previous earnings for workers at lower earnings levels. For example, benefits for someone who earned about 45 percent of the average wage and then retired at age sixty-five in 2015 replace about 52 percent of his or her prior earnings. But benefits for a person who always earned the maximum taxable amount replace only about 25 percent of his or her prior earnings, though they are larger in dollar terms than those for the lower-wage worker.

Consider our examples of Ron and Marcie. Ron's monthly benefit of $2,538 is higher than Marcie's benefit of $1,875. However, his benefit only replaces 32.7 percent of his average monthly earnings when he was working. Marcie, on the other hand, replaces 44.4 percent of her average monthly earnings.

Why the Windfall Elimination Provision?

Up until 1983, if your primary job wasn't covered by Social Security (for example, if you worked for the federal government), but then you switched to a job that *was* covered by Social Security, you'd be treated by the SSA as if you were simply another long-term low-wage worker. You had a lot of zeros on your earning record, so your AIME would be low. But oddly, this gave you an advantage. You received a higher percentage of your Social Security–covered income than would someone who had a higher primary insurance amount (PIA), plus you received a pension from your primary job.

Cost-of-Living Adjustment

Unlike your 401(k) or pension (if you're lucky enough to have these things), Social Security benefits are adjusted for inflation. This can be especially important in times of economic turmoil, when too often your investments are at the mercy of the markets. During the Great Recession of 2008, many couples lost much or all of their retirement savings when the stock market crashed. But Social Security was unaffected by the downturn.

The way the Windfall Elimination Provision works is that the 90 percent element of the SSA's formula is reduced and phased in for workers who reach sixty-two or became disabled between 1986 and 1989. In some instances, the 90 percent can be reduced to as little as 40 percent.

The effect of this is to level the playing field a bit. The formula the SSA uses is based on the number of taxed years you worked (that is the number of years you were taxed for Social Security—this is referred to as "substantial earnings").

NUMBER OF YEARS OF SUBSTANTIAL EARNINGS	PERCENTAGE USED IN SSA FORMULA
30+	90
29	85
28	80
27	75
26	70
25	65
24	60
23	55
22	50
21	45
20 or fewer	40

However—and this is an important qualification of this rule—your benefit under the Windfall Elimination Provision can't be reduced to less than half the size of the pension you receive from the time you worked for a non–Social Security taxing company.

The Importance of Social Security for Minorities

Because many minorities tend to be part of the lower-earning section of the population, Social Security takes on a special importance for them. In 2012, the Social Security Administration conducted a survey of the "Income of the Population, 55 or Older." They found that for beneficiaries aged sixty-five and older, Social Security benefits represent at least 90 percent of the income received by 44 percent of Asian Americans, 46 percent of African Americans, and 53 percent of Hispanics. That's compared with only 35 percent of whites.

As well, the Windfall Elimination Provision doesn't apply to you if:

- You're a federal worker and were first hired after December 31, 1983.
- You were employed on December 31, 1983, by a nonprofit that at first didn't withhold Social Security payroll taxes but later did.
- Your only pension is for working on the railroad.
- Your only work on which you didn't pay payroll taxes for Social Security was before 1957.
- You have thirty or more years of substantial earnings covered by Social Security.

GOVERNMENT PENSION OFFSET

If You Used to Work for the Government

Pensions, although increasingly disappearing from private companies, are still very much around in federal, state, and local government jobs. It's possible, given the financial crisis that seems to be gripping most states and big cities, that in time many of these may also vanish. But for right now the Social Security Administration needs rules in place to deal with them. We've already seen one such rule: the Windfall Elimination Provision. Now we're about to look at another: the Government Pension Offset.

WHO IT AFFECTS

This provision is aimed at people taking spousal benefits and benefits for widows and widowers. If you're in this category and have a pension from the government (federal, state, or local; doesn't make a difference) the SSA will reduce your benefits by two-thirds of your pension.

"Social Security is not a retirement savings plan; it is a social insurance program. It's a contract that says, as a society, we will look out for you and your family when you can no longer work."

—Jeff Bingaman, former U.S. senator

Consider Martha. Her husband, Randall, died, leaving her a widow at age sixty-four. Her survivors benefit ought to be $700 a month. But Martha, when she was younger, worked for the U.S. Postal Service. Her pension payment from the postal service comes to $600. Two-thirds of that is $400, so the SSA reduces her monthly survivors benefit to $300 a month ($700 − $400 = $300). Even if Martha chooses to take her postal service pension in a single lump sum, it won't make a difference; the SSA will calculate what her monthly payments would have been and reduce her survivor payments accordingly.

When Benefits Are Offset

When Social Security first started, it was common for the man to be the bread-winner of the family and for the woman to stay home. Now, of course, that's no longer the case. In order to hold the line of its costs, the Social Security system offsets survivors or spousal benefits if they're lower than the spouse or widow's (or widower's) own benefits. For instance, as the SSA explains in a paper (available on their website), "If a woman worked and earned her own $800 monthly Social Security benefit, but was also due a $500 wife's benefit on her husband's record, we couldn't pay that wife's benefit because her own benefit offset it."

Exceptions to the Government Pension Offset Rule

There are some circumstances in which even if you have a government pension your spousal or survivors benefits won't be reduced. These include:

- If you get a government pension that's not based on your earnings
- If in addition to getting your pension, you paid Social Security taxes on your government job. This includes the further conditions that:

- You filed for and were entitled to spousal or survivors benefits before April 1, 2004, or
- The last day you had the job from which you're entitled to a pension was before July 1, 2004, or
- You paid Social Security taxes during the last sixty days you worked for the government

- You switched from the Civil Service Retirement System (CSRS) to the Federal Employees' Retirement System (FERS) after December 31, 1987. In addition:

    - You have to have filed for and be entitled to your spousal or survivors benefits before April 1, 2004, or
    - Your last day of working for the government was before July 1, 2004, or
    - You paid payroll taxes to Social Security for sixty months or more sometime after January 1988

- You received (or were eligible to do so) your government pension before December 1982 and were also eligible for spousal benefits under the rules prevailing on January 1977
- You received a government pension before July 1, 1983, and were already receiving one-half support from your spouse

Whew! That's a lot of rules to take in. The basic point to come away with from all this is that if you get a government pension, it's going to affect your benefits. Overall, you'll still get money from the government, but you won't get your full Social Security benefit.

THE RETROACTIVE LUMP-SUM OPTION

Getting a Chunk of Money All at Once

Applying for your benefits as soon as you reach your full retirement age (FRA) is a sound strategy for maximizing the amount of your monthly check (assuming you don't want to wait until you turn seventy). However, you may want to wait a bit longer past FRA before you apply for benefits. Specifically, you may want to take advantage of a little-known option called the retroactive lump sum. This option allows you to receive a number of months of retroactive benefits in one lump sum. That is, you get a bunch of cash right up front.

Here's how it works.

GETTING A CHUNK OF CHANGE

Let's imagine that in 2017 Anne reaches her full retirement age of sixty-six. She's entitled to a monthly benefit of $1,758. However, rather than immediately applying for benefits, Anne elects to wait a year. By doing this, she may qualify for a retroactive lump-sum payment of up to six months' worth of benefits—$10,548.

Downsides

This option can make sense if you've received some bad health news and don't believe you'll live very long but want to pay down some debt immediately. It can also make sense if you want to take that money and invest it. However, be aware that many—in fact, most—people who take this benefit with investing in mind don't, in fact, invest the money. Rather, they spend it on various immediate necessities, and before they know it, the money's gone.

"You can look at history of these things, and Social Security wasn't devised to be a system that supported you for a thirty-year retirement after a twenty-five-year career . . . So there will be things that, you know, the retirement age has to be changed, maybe some of the benefits have to be affected, maybe some of the inflation adjustments have to be revised."

—Lloyd Blankfein, American business executive

There is another downside that is not readily apparent. When you take a retroactive lump sum, the SSA fixes your regular monthly benefit back to the date where the lump-sum payout began accruing. In Anne's case, she took a six-month lump-sum payout when she was at FRA plus one year. In other words, for Anne, her monthly benefit will now be calculated as if she had started taking it at age sixty-six and a half (not sixty-seven). Another significant consideration is that the retroactive lump-sum payment boosts your provisional income for the year, potentially taking you into a higher tax bracket such that some significant portion of your benefits will be taxed.

Who Can Claim This?

Despite the downsides, receiving a lump sum totaling six months' worth of benefits understandably has a lot of appeal. Unfortunately, Social Security has a complicated set of provisions for who can take what amount, and when:

- If you were born on or before April 30, 1950, you can claim the retroactive lump-sum benefit and (very significantly) you can make it retroactive to any point after you reached your full retirement age.
- If you were born after April 30, 1950, you can still take the lump-sum benefit, but you can only make it retroactive to six months before you file.

It's worth noting that if you reached full retirement age on or before April 30, 2016, and have filed and suspended your benefits (you may remember from earlier that the file and suspend strategy is no longer allowed under new Social Security rules), you have much greater flexibility in taking the lump-sum benefit, with the understanding that doing so will freeze your benefit amount at whatever point you take the retroactive payment. Following is an example of how this might work in the real world.

Social Security in Germany

Germany in some respects is the home of social security systems, since the original idea of social insurance began with Chancellor Otto von Bismarck. To qualify, you must be at least sixty-five years old with at least five years of contributions to the system. If you're disabled, you may qualify to receive benefits at age sixty-three. There are also provisions for survivors' coverage, orphans, and permanent disability. These are all funded by joint contributions of employee and employer.

Barry was born on January 1, 1948. His primary insurance amount (PIA), that is, the amount of his benefit upon reaching his full retirement age of sixty-six, will be $2,024. In 2014, at age sixty-six, he filed for benefits and then suspended them. Now, two years later in 2016, he anticipates a sudden onset of debt, related to a health emergency. He files for a retroactive lump-sum benefit and requests that it be considered retroactive to the point he reached his full retirement age. His lump-sum payment will be $48,576 ($2,024 × 24 months). However, his monthly benefit, which he now starts receiving, will be $2,024. If he hadn't taken the retroactive lump-sum benefit and instead had simply started his benefits in 2016, he'd be receiving $2,361 (because his PIA increases by 8 percent each year he doesn't take benefits).

Still, even though his monthly benefits aren't as high as they'd have been if he'd delayed taking them, Barry may have made the right choice. His lump-sum payment will go a long way to paying down some medical bills and prevent him from sinking into ruinous debt.

STOPPING YOUR BENEFITS

The Strategy of Waiting

Let's consider Norman. He's sixty-two and has been working at the same company for most of his life. Now, with his wife retired and his children moved away and with children of their own, he's ready to close up his cubicle and retire. He knows he's retiring before his full retirement age, but his monthly benefit of $1,845 seems fine. In addition, his wife's Social Security benefits and careful withdrawals from their savings should enable them to live a reasonably comfortable lifestyle. He announces his retirement to his boss and applies for benefits.

Six months go by. Norman is happy, although he wishes sometimes that money wasn't so tight. Then, he gets a call from his old boss. It seems the company has taken on a new project. It's expected to take about five years to complete, and the boss wants to know if Norman would come back and work on it at his old salary.

What to do?

STOPPING BENEFITS BEFORE YOUR FRA

Norman knows that if he continues to take benefits while going back to work, he'll exceed his provisional income limits to the point that his benefits will, effectively, disappear. However, the job offer is too good to turn down. Luckily, since Norman took his benefits before his FRA, and because it's been less than a year since he filed, he has the option of stopping his benefits. The downside is that Norman is going to have to repay to the Social Security Administration the six months' worth of benefits he's already received—that is, $11,070. Moreover, Norman's repayment must include any other benefits received by his family that were the result of his filing (spousal benefits, children's benefits, etc.). The SSA makes sure that there are no surprises to these family members: Anyone who received such benefits and is now repaying them must sign a form consenting to Norman's withdrawal of his request for benefits.

How Are We Compared to the World?

As of June 2015, the average Social Security benefit amounted to about $16,000 a year ($1,335 per month). How does that compare to other programs around the world? The answer is, not very well. Out of thirty-four countries, the United States ranked thirty-first in benefits as a percentage of earnings. The top five nations are:

- Netherlands
- Israel
- Denmark
- Austria
- Spain

The lowest nation in this list is Japan.

All of this certainly presents Norman and his wife with some challenges. But the upside is that now he can wait until he reaches his full retirement age to start claiming benefits again, at which point his benefit will have grown 8 percent per year to a nice $2,508 per month. He'll be getting almost $8,000 per year more in benefits when he retires at his full retirement age of sixty-six.

AT FULL RETIREMENT AGE

Suppose Norman had retired at sixty-three but didn't receive the offer from his old boss until he'd passed his sixty-sixth birthday. What then?

Norman could have requested a voluntary suspension of benefits. He could do this up to the age of seventy, after which he'd have to continue to take benefits and couldn't stop them.

"The economist John Maynard Keynes said that in the long run, we are all dead. If he were around today he might say that, in the long run, we are all on Social Security and Medicare."

—Ben Bernanke, American economist and former chairman
of the Federal Reserve

The great advantage of taking a voluntary suspension when you've suddenly got a new source of income is that you start accumulating those delayed retirement credits that lead to an increase in your benefit. There are some significant advantages in doing this, since later in your life is when you're likely to need a higher benefit to cope with medical expenses. However, and this is very important, under the new rules for Social Security passed in 2015, once you suspend your retirement benefits you are deemed by the SSA to have suspended *all* benefits, including spousal, family, and anything else you've claimed. Furthermore, if you voluntarily suspend your benefits, any benefits you receive that are based on someone else's earnings record will be suspended. You should certainly take this into consideration when debating whether or not to stop your benefits.

The Month After

The Social Security Administration notes: "We pay Social Security benefits the month after they are due. If you contact us in June and request that we suspend benefits, you will still receive your June benefit payment in July."

APPEALING AN SSA DECISION

Getting the System to Change Its Mind

With such a complex system involving so many people, it's inevitable that many of the Social Security Administration's decisions are going to be unpopular with applicants. Here we'll look at how you can appeal an SSA decision.

DISABILITY BENEFITS

Probably the biggest area for disagreement between the SSA and the general population lies in the area of disability benefits. This is especially true because, if you remember, the SSA looks not just at whether your disability prevents you from doing your old job but whether it also prevents you from doing any related jobs that require similar experience and/or training. It's possible that the SSA has denied you disability benefits on the grounds that even though you can't do your old job, there are still several related jobs they believe you can perform. You, on the other hand, with a more intimate knowledge of what's actually involved in the job, disagree.

You can file your appeal online at https://secure.ssa.gov/iApplsRe/start. Doing so will speed up the process of the appeal, ensuring a more timely decision from the SSA. If the SSA denies your benefits, they will notify you by letter. They assume their letter takes five days to be delivered, and you have sixty days from receipt of that letter to file an appeal.

Levels of Appeal

There are four levels of appeal:

1. Reconsideration
2. Hearing before an administrative law judge
3. Review by the Appeals Council
4. Hearing in a federal court

Reconsideration

In this stage, someone who wasn't involved in the original consideration of your claim goes over your application and the reason it was denied. Although few claims are reinstated at this stage, it's important to make sure that your claim wasn't denied because of a simple administrative glitch. As with your initial appeal, if the Reconsideration stage denies your claim you have sixty days from the receipt of the SSA's letter to file an appeal to the next stage.

Timely Appeal

If you miss the sixty-day window to file an appeal, that in itself may be used by the SSA as a basis for denial of your claim. There are some exceptions to this, but they're few and far between. In short, if you miss your appeal deadline, you'd better have a very good reason that you can back up with proof. Otherwise your appeals process will be stopped dead in its tracks.

Hearing Before an Administrative Law Judge

The date of the hearing will be set by the judge's office based on her or his schedule. It may be anywhere from several months to a year from the filing of the claim. The judge's office will send you a letter at least twenty days before the hearing, letting you know its time and place. Usually it will be within seventy-five miles of where you live. If you still have trouble traveling to the meeting, notify the SSA and inform them of that fact. If the reason is medical, send along a doctor's report confirming it. It's possible in many instances to hold the hearing by video so you can remain in the comfort of your own home. If the hearing is, for some reason, more than seventy-five miles from your home, the SSA may pay your transportation costs and even, subject to the approval of the judge, such expenses as meals and lodgings. For all these things you'll need to submit a written report to the judge at the hearing or as soon as possible afterward.

Faxing the Evidence

According to the SSA website, "If your case is electronic, evidence can be faxed into the claim file using a special fax number and bar code provided by the hearing office or sent by your representative through Electronic Records Express (ERE) at www.ssa.gov/ere."

Given that this is a formal hearing, most experts strongly recommend that you be accompanied by a lawyer and that you bring all of your documentation of your disability with you. This documentation can include such things as:

- Medical records
- Affidavits from doctors and/or therapists
- Prescription receipts
- Records of hospital stays

Whenever possible, bring the originals of these documents. As well, bring any additional evidence you'd like the judge to consider in making her decision.

Since the SSA is highly experienced in its own rules and regulations, to say nothing of handling thousands of appeals such as yours, its representatives at the hearing will be experienced and knowledgeable. Look for a lawyer who's handled Social Security appeals before. Remember, this is an important financial issue for you, and you won't help yourself by being cheap in the matter of legal representation.

When the judge asks you questions about your case, you will be under oath, and your testimony, as well as the rest of the proceedings, will be recorded. After the hearing, the judge will issue a written opinion upholding or denying your claim.

Tell the SSA about Your Lawyer

If you're going to bring a lawyer with you to the hearing, the Social Security Administration wants to know about it. Fill out form SSA-1696-U4 Appointment of a Representative and send it in before the hearing.

Review by the Appeals Council

The Social Security Appeals Council is located in and around the Washington, D.C., area, and filing an appeal before it may involve traveling there. As with the administrative hearing, it's important to submit any new evidence and to make your case clearly and succinctly in writing (your lawyer can help you with this).

The council will consider your case and decide if the administrative hearing made a mistake in rejecting your claim. If they choose that course of action, they can either decide the matter for themselves or send it back to the administrative judge for further consideration.

Hearing in a Federal Court

Your court of last appeal, so to speak, is the federal court. This can be an extremely expensive process, and you shouldn't undertake it lightly. But if you feel that everyone in the appeals process thus far has misjudged your case, you have this option open to you.

BE FAIR TO YOURSELF AND OTHERS

Appealing a claim, whether it is for a disability or something else in the Social Security system, can be an emotional business. There's potentially a lot of money at stake for you and your family, after all. In many respects, we're talking about your whole future. For that reason:

- **Be fair.** No one in the Social Security Administration is consciously trying to cheat you out of something that's yours. The SSA doesn't take some perverse pleasure in denying claims. It's just their responsibility to see that the system is administered fairly and that the government's money isn't wasted.
- **Be calm.** Even though you may be upset if the tone of a hearing isn't in your favor, yelling and screaming isn't going to accomplish anything, beyond probably ensuring that your claim will be denied.
- **Be detailed and thorough.** Take what time you need to gather the evidence for your appeals process. It's far better to have too much evidence than too little.

HEALTH AND SOCIAL SECURITY

Healthcare in Your Golden Years

Healthcare and Social Security may seem like two different topics, but they're intimately connected to one another. Healthcare is probably the single biggest expense you'll have as you grow older. Medical science keeps finding ways to keep us living longer. That's nice, but that also means we have to find ways of stretching out our savings and ensuring we have access to medical care. As we've stressed throughout this book, the issue of life expectancy is among the most important factors in considering your Social Security benefits and how they fit in with the rest of your retirement savings plan.

WHERE DOES HEALTHCARE STAND IN THE UNITED STATES

Sadly, even after many years of debate and discussion and trying various ways of providing healthcare to its population, the United States ranks dead last among wealthy nations when it comes to a number of healthcare metrics (including quality, access, efficiency, equity, and healthy lives). This assessment is not hearsay, but comes from a 2014 study by the Commonwealth Fund, a private foundation dedicated to supporting research on healthcare issues.

It will take some time to fully evaluate the effects of the Affordable Care Act (a.k.a. Obamacare), but it seems clear that healthcare issues will continue to be a political football for some time to come.

One thing most people *seem* to agree on, though, is that they want Medicare left alone.

MEDICARE: WHERE'D IT COME FROM?

Medicare is much more recent than most of the Social Security system. It started out as a way for the government to provide medical care to the families of those serving in the armed forces. This was accomplished through the Dependents' Medical Care Act of 1956. Then, in 1965, President Lyndon Johnson signed Medicare into law as part of Title XVIII of the Social Security Act. The program's stated intention was to offer medical care to people sixty-five and older.

Medicare and Civil Rights

Medicare played a role in the 1960s burgeoning civil rights struggle by declaring it would only pay health providers if they integrated their facilities.

The program is administered through the Centers for Medicare and Medicaid Services, but the Social Security Administration is bound up with it. Indeed, a great deal of information about Medicare is available on the SSA's website, www.ssa.gov. Basically, the SSA determines if you're eligible for Medicare and decides if you're entitled to a Low-Income Subsidy (also called Extra Help). We'll talk more about that in a bit.

The Medicare program has expanded a number of times over the years, the most recent being coverage of most prescription drugs in 2003 under President George W. Bush.

WHAT DOES IT DO?

Medicare offers health insurance to those sixty-five and older. It also provides coverage for people with disabilities, kidney failure, and amyotrophic lateral sclerosis, better known as Lou Gehrig's disease. It covers more than 48 million people, although, as we'll see, it doesn't cover all medical expenses. Nonetheless, for millions of people it's their primary means of medical insurance.

It's divided into four parts, which are called, somewhat unimaginatively, Part A, Part B, Part C, and Part D. These are usually characterized as follows:

- Part A is called Hospital Insurance.
- Part B is called Medical Insurance.
- Part C is called Medicare Advantage Plans, or fee-for-service.
- Part D is called prescription drug coverage.

We'll look at all of these in greater detail in the next chapter.

MEDICAID

Along with Medicare, the other prong of Social Security–related government healthcare is Medicaid. This program is designed to offer healthcare benefits to low-income families. It significantly expanded under Obamacare.

Medicaid is a product of President Lyndon Johnson's Great Society, the series of social reforms he launched in his first full term. In 1965, Congress added Title XIX to the Social Security Act, under which states were to receive matching funds from the federal government to provide medical care to families unable to pay for it themselves. Thus, Medicaid is funded at both the federal and state levels.

And although it's a federal program, Medicaid is largely administered at the state level. Currently Medicaid provides care for about 60 million people. Unlike Social Security, Medicaid isn't just for people of a certain age; its beneficiaries include children and young people.

Medicaid is a means-tested system, as you'd expect of a program designed to help those with low incomes. States decide on their own eligibility criteria but must keep them within federal guidelines. Generally, the system considers income in relationship to the federal poverty level, which, as of 2016, is $24,250 for a family of four (this figure is updated every year to take inflation into account).

We'll come back to Medicaid later on. Right now, let's talk about how you qualify for Medicare.

Medigap

Because Medicare does not cover all medical procedures, many people purchase insurance plans to deal with the gaps in coverage. These plans are known as Medigap.

WHO'S ELIGIBLE FOR MEDICARE?

The most basic thing you must do to qualify for Medicare is live until you're sixty-five. You must also be a U.S. citizen or have been a legal resident for at least five years. You or your spouse must have paid Medicare taxes for at least ten years.

You can get Medicare benefits if you're younger than sixty-five provided that you're disabled and have been receiving SSDI benefits or Railroad Retirement disability benefits for at least twenty-four months. You can also qualify if you have end-stage renal disease or need a kidney transplant.

More Information

To find out more about what is covered by Medicare, call 1-800-633-4227 and ask for publication CMS-10050. You can also order a copy at www.medicare .gov.

Who Pays?

Medicare is paid for through payroll taxes in the same way as Social Security. As well, monthly premiums are deducted from Social Security checks. Currently, both employer and employee pay a tax of 1.45 percent. (If you're self-employed, you must pay a tax of 2.9 percent.) This tax primarily pays for Part A of Medicare. The other parts are paid for through premiums paid by those enrolled in Medicare, as well as by the government's general fund. As with most other things connected to retirement, the system is expected to experience strain as baby boomers retire. The Henry J. Kaiser Family Foundation estimates that Medicare spending will grow to $1 trillion by 2022. As with Social Security retirement benefits, though, there are a number of possible ways to deal with this growth in spending. Among them:

- Increase Medicare taxes
- Institute means testing, as is done for Medicaid

- Link Medicare to life expectancy
- Move toward online doctor visits rather than actual visits

Eventually some combination of these approaches, as well as others, will probably fix the issue of increased Medicare costs.

MEDICARE

Your Health in Retirement

As we said previously, Medicare is divided into four parts. We'll consider each of these in turn in this chapter. To begin with, let's start by looking at what Medicare covers.

PART A

Part A of Medicare, which focuses on hospital stays, covers the following:

- Semiprivate room
- Meals
- Nursing
- Hospital services

For a stay in the hospital of one to sixty days, you pay up to $952. For the next thirty days, you pay $228 per day. From day ninety-one to day 150, you pay $456 per day. For anything in excess of 150 days, you are responsible for all costs of the stay.

If, after three days in the hospital, you are moved to a skilled nursing facility, Medicare pays for the following:

- A semiprivate room
- Meals
- Nursing
- Rehabilitation
- Miscellaneous services

For the first twenty days in such a facility, you pay nothing. For days twenty-one through 100, you pay up to $114 per day. After that, you pay all costs associated with remaining in the facility.

Medicare will also pay for some home-based healthcare services. These include:

- Part-time skilled nursing care
- Home health aide services
- Physical and occupational therapy
- Speech therapy
- Certain medical equipment, such as wheelchairs, crutches, walkers, etc.

You pay 20 percent of the cost of medical equipment. All providers of such equipment and other services have to be certified by Medicare.

It's possible that if you have a terminal illness, you'll be placed in hospice care. Medicare Part A will cover the following elements of that care:

- Doctors' services
- Nursing
- Medical equipment
- Medical supplies
- Drugs to control your symptoms (you pay up to $5 for each prescription drug)
- Short-term hospital stay
- Therapy, both physical and speech
- Social worker services
- Dietary counseling
- Grief counseling for you and your family

Blood Is Covered

When you're in the hospital or a skilled nursing facility, it may be necessary for you to undergo a blood transfusion. If that's the case, Medicare Part A will pay for the blood after the first three pints. However, if you or someone you know donates three pints of blood, Medicare will pay for all the blood.

PART B

If you enroll in Part B of Medicare, you'll pay a monthly premium, just as you would for any insurance. As of 2016, the standard premium is $121.80. If you get Social Security benefits, Railroad Retirement benefits, or Office of Personnel Management benefits, the premium will be deducted from the benefits. Otherwise, Medicare will send you a monthly bill.

If your income is above a certain amount, the size of your premium increases. The following table, adapted slightly from www .medicare.gov, shows how this increase works.

ANNUAL INCOME		YOU PAY
File Individual Tax Return	**File Joint Tax Return**	**Monthly Premium**
$85,000 or less	$170,000 or less	$121.80
Above $85,000 up to $107,000	Above $170,000 up to $214,000	$170.50
Above $107,000 up to $160,000	Above $214,000 up to $320,000	$243.60
Above $160,000 up to $214,000	Above $320,000 up to $428,000	$316.70
Above $214,000	Above $428,000	$389.80

What Does It Cover?

Part B of Medicare is designed to cover doctor visits and every-day medical care. To this end, it will pay for:

- Visits to doctors who accept Medicare patients; this includes visits to hospitals, clinics, doctors' offices, or care in your home
- Medical equipment, on the same order as what's covered in Part A
- Tests done outside hospitals
- Preventive measures (for example, flu shots or vaccines)
- Visits to the emergency room
- Outpatient care and some inpatient care (for instance, if you're being kept under observation at a hospital)
- Ambulance and air rescue services
- Health counseling for lifestyle changes (giving up smoking or drinking, for example, or losing weight)

Medicare Abroad

Save for very rare circumstances, Medicare does not cover medical services performed out of the United States. This is an important consideration for anyone contemplating retiring abroad. On the other hand, many destination countries for retirees have free or very inexpensive healthcare, so the loss of Medicare benefits doesn't matter much. If you're thinking of retiring abroad, be sure to check the status of healthcare in the country to which you're planning to retire.

PART C

This is often referred to as Medicare Advantage. It's a place where the government system of Medicare touches the private insurance business.

If you enroll in Medicare C, you sign up for a plan run by a private company. Pretty much, these plans will cover the same things as Medicare Parts A and B, but you may find that there are some advantages to the private plans. For example, they may charge you lower copays. The important thing is to pick the plan that works best for you.

Keep in mind that where you live will have something to do with the Medicare Advantage plan you choose (assuming you decide to go that route). In some rural areas, there aren't many plans available. People living in urban areas are likely to have many choices when it comes to medical insurance.

It's Not Written in Stone

If, having signed up for Part A and B, you change your mind and decide you'd rather go with one of the private plans in Part C, that's fine. You can switch. Or the other way around. Either way, it's all good!

The bulk of plans in Medicare Advantage are health maintenance organizations (HMOs) or preferred provider organizations (PPOs). Just like other kinds of healthcare insurance, they'll come with a list of doctors participating in their plan; if you see someone outside the network, you'll pay extra. One good thing about Medicare Advantage is that it caps the annual amount you'll spend out of pocket, something Medicare Parts A and B don't do. So if you're concerned about your annual healthcare costs as well as your copay (in other words, you anticipate frequent visits to the doctor during the year), Part C may be the way to go. However, one thing to keep in mind is that like any private plan, those healthcare providers that are participants in Part C can go away—that is, they can decide to withdraw from participation in Part C. If that happens, you'll have to go back to Part A and B Medicare, at least until you can find another provider or insurer.

Enrolling in Medicare

You can sign up for Medicare starting three months before the date you turn sixty-five and ending four months after that date. Thereafter, you can sign up between January 1 and March 31 of each year. *But*—very important!—if you don't sign up for Part B when you first become eligible for it, your premiums will go up 10 percent for every twelve months you don't sign up thereafter. And that hike in your premiums will last you the rest of your life! So if you do nothing else in that initial seven months around your sixty-fifth birthday, sign up for Part B.

PART D

As mentioned previously, Part D of Medicare is concerned with drug prescriptions. This is certainly an increasingly large part of any retiree's life. As with Part B, you pay a monthly premium. Plan D plans vary from state to state, as do the premiums, but they generally range from $35 to $50 per month. There is also some variation in which drugs are covered by the plan.

Under Part D, you're required to pay whatever deductible your plan has (though some plans have no deductible). As well, you are responsible for copays until their total reaches a specific number ($3,310 in 2016). When you hit that number, you fall into what's called the "doughnut hole." In the doughnut hole, you must pay 45 percent of the cost of brand-name drugs and 65 percent of the cost of generic drugs. When all of your out-of-pocket costs for the year hit $4,850, you get out of the hole and go into catastrophic protection, during which 95 percent of your expenditures are paid by Medicare. When you reach the end of the year, the system resets and you start over again.

Sign Up for Part D

Just as with Part B, you're eligible to sign up for Part D starting three months before your sixty-fifth birthday and ending four months after it. If you don't sign up in that initial period, your premium will go up—and stay that way. So as with Part B, sign up for Part D as soon as you become eligible.

The open enrollment period for Plan D lasts from October 15 to December 7 every year.

WHAT MEDICARE DOESN'T COVER

Although Medicare will pay an awful lot of your expenses in retirement, it doesn't cover some things. These are expenses that you'll wind up paying out of your own pocket. They include:

- **Glasses and eye care.** Medicare won't cover the cost of new frames and lenses or eye examinations. Nor does it cover the cost of contact lenses.

- **Dental care.** Although Medicare will cover some dental operations (usually ones that are performed while you're in the hospital), it won't cover routine visits to the dentist. Nor does it cover dentures.
- **Hearing aids.** Medicare won't cover routine hearing exams or the charge of getting and maintaining hearing aids.
- **Cosmetic surgery.** Medicare won't cover cosmetic surgery, including breast enlargement or reduction, unless it's the result of an illness or accident.
- **Acupuncture.** Even though it's widely used in Chinese medicine, Medicare says no to acupuncture.

Chiropractors

Chiropractic care is covered under Part B—sort of. The manipulation of your spine, provided the service is given by a licensed chiropractor, is covered. You pay 20 percent of the cost plus your deductible. Medicare does *not* pay for tests, including x-rays, and therapy.

EXTRA HELP WITH PRESCRIPTION COSTS

If Drugs Are Too Expensive

Even with Medicare helping out, some medical costs are still soaring. One of the most pervasive of these is what we pay for prescription drugs. In the United States, the average person spends about $1,000 a year for prescribed medications. In Canada, the next highest spender, the average citizen pays about $600.

Part of this is because we use a lot more pharmaceuticals than the rest of the world. If you've got a condition, there's probably a pill you can take for it. Another reason is that in the United States drugs cost a lot more—sometimes as much as 50 or 60 percent what they cost in places like France or Germany—because the pharmaceutical industry in America is unregulated in regard to price.

The Most Hated Man in America

In September 2015 Martin Shkreli, former CEO of Turing Pharmaceuticals, acquired a license to manufacture Daraprim, a drug used to combat malaria and other parasitic-based infections. It is also used in the treatment of certain diseases that appear in AIDS patients. Shkreli raised the price of the drug from $13.50 to $750—a rise of more than 5,000 percent. For his action and his arrogance when challenged about it, news media characterized him as "the most hated man in America." Ironically, several months later he was arrested by the FBI on charges of securities fraud. (Although Turing indicated it would lower the cost of Daraprim, it has not yet done so; a monthly course of treatment costs $75,000.)

HOW CAN I GET EXTRA HELP?

Recognizing these problems, Medicare offers help with paying the cost of prescription drugs. However, this assistance is only given to people with low incomes who might not be expected to afford the medicine that many of them need.

This financial assistance, worth approximately $4,000 per year, includes things such as prescription copays, monthly premiums, and deductibles. To qualify for this assistance:

- You must be a resident of the United States.
- Your resources must be lower than $13,640 for an individual and $27,250 for a couple. By "resources" the SSA means any stocks or bonds you hold, and any money in your bank account(s). However, they don't include your house, car, or life insurance policy.
- Your annual income must be equal to or less than $17,820 for an individual and $24,030 for a couple.

As with most other Social Security–based programs, you can apply for this assistance online by downloading and filling out SSA's Application for Extra Help with Medicare Prescription Drug Plan Costs (SSA-1020). You can also call the agency at 1-800-772-1213.

Avoid the Penalty

As previously mentioned, failure to enroll on time in Medicare Part D, the prescription drug part of the program, results in a penalty. However, if you apply for and receive Extra Help, that penalty won't apply.

A Little Bit of Extra Help

Even if your income or resources exceeds the limits outlined by the prescription drug assistance program, it's possible you could qualify for some extra financial help with your prescriptions. If you or your spouse give financial support to someone else (typically a child or a parent), or if you live in Alaska or Hawaii, you may qualify for the Low-Income Subsidy, or Extra Help, program. It's something worth discussing with your local Social Security office.

MEDICARE SAVINGS PROGRAMS

While applying for Extra Help, you might also want to consider applying for the Medicare Savings Programs. These are administered by the states and are a way for you to save for anticipated medical expenses. When you fill out and return the form for Extra Help, the state automatically sends you information about the Medicare Savings Programs, unless you ask it not to.

There are four kinds of Medicare Savings Programs:

1. Qualified Medicare Beneficiary program
2. Specified Low-Income Medicare Beneficiary program
3. Qualifying Individual program
4. Qualified Disabled and Working Individuals program

If you qualify for any of these, you automatically qualify for Extra Help in paying for your prescription drugs.

Qualified Medicare Beneficiary Program (QMB)

To qualify for this savings program, your monthly income must be equal to or less than $1,010 if you're single or $1,355 if you're married. Your resources must amount to no more than $7,280 if you're single or $10,930 if you're a couple. The program helps pay for Part A and Part B premiums as well as deductibles and copayments.

Specified Low-Income Medicare Beneficiary Program (SLMB)

To qualify for SLMB, your monthly income cannot exceed $1,208 (if you're married, the limit is $1,622) and your resources must be at or below $7,280 ($10,930 for married couples). SLMB helps pay for Medicare Part B expenses but none of the other parts. If you qualify for SLMB, you automatically get help with Part D, prescription drugs.

Qualifying Individual Program (QI)

Unlike the two programs just noted, you must apply for QI benefits every year; each year, priority will be given to those applicants who received QI benefits the previous year. If you qualify for Medicaid, you're ineligible for QI benefits. To qualify for QI benefits, you must be limited to a monthly income of $1,357, or, if you're a married couple, to $1,823. As well, your resources cannot total more than $7,280 if you're single or $10,930 if you're a married couple. The program helps pay for Part B expenses only, but as with QMB and SLMB, if you qualify for QI, you automatically qualify for assistance for Part D.

Qualified Disabled and Working Individuals Program (QDWI)

To qualify for this program, you must:

- Be a working disabled person younger than sixty-five

- Not be getting medical assistance from the state in which you live
- Have lost your Part A coverage because you went back to work

In addition, you must have a monthly income at or below $4,045 as an individual or $5,425 if you're part of a married couple. Your resources must not exceed $4,000 for individuals and $6,000 for married couples.

The program helps recipients pay for Part A, and as with the other three programs, if you qualify for it, you automatically qualify for Part D assistance.

If you think you qualify for one or more of these programs, call your state Medicaid program.

MEDICARE ADVANTAGE

Independent Insurance Plans

If you go to Medicare's website (www.medicare.gov), you'll find a button that reads, "Find health & drug plans." Clicking on that will take you to Medicare's plan finder, which is the easiest and best way to compare private health insurance plans that are available to you through Medicare Advantage.

PRIVATE PLANS

We discussed Medicare Advantage a bit earlier in this book. As you may remember, this is the name given to Part C of Medicare, and it gives the option of signing on to a private medical plan rather than traditional Medicare, embodied in Parts A and B.

The first challenge to those interested in enrolling in Medicare Advantage is to choose between the wide variety of plans on offer (although in some areas of the country, there is much less variety, making your choice easier although at the same time restricting your options). When you click on the "Find health & drug plans" button, you will go to the Medicare Plan Finder, where you can discover the plans available to you.

Plan Ratings

The Medicare Plan Finder also gives the plans a rating. If a plan is accompanied by a red warning sign, this means it's had low-quality ratings for three years in a row. You probably want to avoid such plans.

Clicking Through the Plans

Once on the Medicare Plan Finder page, enter your zip code to begin the process. You'll begin a four-step process:

1. First, the site will ask you some questions about your current coverage. You'll be asked if you currently have Original (or Traditional) Medicare, if you are on a Medicare Health Plan, and so on. You are also asked about the sort of help you get from Medicare to pay for your prescription drugs.

2. Next, you'll be asked to enter the names and dosages of the drugs that are currently prescribed for you.

3. In the next step, you'll be asked to choose the pharmacy or pharmacies where you would like to pick up your prescriptions. It's a good idea to enter at least two, so you can compare prices.

4. Finally, you're given an opportunity to refine your search. For example, you can ask for a listing of plans with low monthly premiums, and you can determine the parameters of those premiums. You can also ask for plans offered by a particular company or companies.

Once you've gone through all these steps and clicked the "Continue to Plan Results" button, the site will show you what plans are available in your area that meet your criteria. The information includes:

- Monthly drug and health premiums
- Deductibles and drug copay/coinsurance costs
- Health benefits, including out-of-pocket spending limits
- An estimate of annual health and drug costs

COMPARING PLANS

How you compare one plan to another depends on your priorities:

- Are you concerned about a high deductible?
- What is the highest monthly premium you can afford?
- Are you mostly concerned with your annual drug costs?

Write out a list of questions. Then, put them in the order of importance they have to you. Side by side, set out the benefits offered by each plan you're considering, again keeping them in their order of importance to you.

Once you've done this, you are a long way toward making your decision. However, before you do so, find out which plan provides the best Part D prescription drug coverage.

Cheap Isn't Always Better

Although you're on a fixed income now, resist the temptation to go for the cheapest healthcare plan. Too often, you get what you pay for, and your health isn't something to take chances with in retirement. As well, don't assume that if a plan is more expensive (for example, it has a higher premium) that it's necessarily better. Focus on the specific benefits and the numbers that are important to you.

Which Doctors?

At some point in your search for the right plan, spend a little time investigating which doctors accept which plans. It won't do you any good if you find a plan that's perfect for you but the only doctor who accepts it is a two-hour drive away. As mentioned earlier, this will be less of a problem for you if you live in an urban area, where there are more doctors to choose from. But if you live in an underpopulated part of the country, look at this question early in your search.

If you decide to enroll in a preferred provider organization (PPO) that allows you to go to any doctor, be aware that you'll have a higher copay for any doctor outside the plan's network. If you already have a doctor, you can call her or him and find out whether she or he accepts the plan you're interested in.

NOW YOU'RE READY TO ENROLL

Once you've picked your plan, there are three different ways to enroll:

1. On the Medicare website, click the "Enroll" button next to the plan you've chosen.
2. Call 1-800-633-4227, and someone from Medicare's help line will walk you through the procedure.
3. Go to the plan's website and sign up there.

If you change your mind and decide you'd prefer to leave your plan and go back to Traditional Medicare (i.e., Parts A and B), you can disenroll. But you must do this during the annual disenrollment period, which is between January 1 and February 14 every year. However, if you signed up for Medicare at age sixty-five and this is your first year in the system, you can disenroll at any point within the first twelve months you signed up. You can also buy a Medigap policy within sixty-three days of ending your Medicare Advantage plan.

It's possible you'll move during retirement and find yourself outside the area covered by your Medicare Advantage plan. No problem. You can re-enroll in a different plan or, if you can't find one you like, you can enroll in Traditional Medicare. You can also change your plan to another plan or to Traditional Medicare if you:

- Receive Extra Help with prescription drug costs
- Move into or leave a skilled nursing facility
- Are a long-term resident in a nursing home

MEDIGAP

Whether you're enrolled in Medicare Advantage or in Traditional Medicare, it's entirely possible that there will be gaps in your coverage. In some cases, these may be things you can live with. In others, because of your past medical history or simply for peace of mind, they are not.

To cover these gaps, you're entitled to purchase supplemental insurance, which is called Medigap. However, you'll have to pay all the costs of a Medigap plan.

Enrolling in a Medigap Plan

The first prerequisite for joining a Medigap plan is that you must be enrolled in Medicare—either in Parts A and B, or in Part C. Medicare breaks down Medigap plans into ten different categories, labeled intermittently A through N. The following chart, found on the Medicare website, shows what these plans cover.

You can buy a Medigap policy in the six-month period immediately after you turn sixty-five and are enrolled in Medicare Part B. If you need to buy such a policy, it's important that you do it then, because after the six months is up, you may not be able to purchase Medigap, and if you are, it will probably cost more.

MEDIGAP BENEFITS	MEDIGAP PLANS									
	A	B	C	D	F	G	K	L	M	N
Part A coinsurance and hospital costs up to an additional 365 days after Med care benefits are used up	Yes	Yes	Yes	Yes	Yes	Yes	Yes	Yes	Yes	Yes
Part B coinsurance or copayment	Yes	Yes	Yes	Yes	Yes	Yes	50%	75%	Yes	Yes
Blood (first 3 pints)	Yes	Yes	Yes	Yes	Yes	Yes	50%	75%	Yes	Yes
Part A hospice care coinsurance or copayment	Yes	Yes	Yes	Yes	Yes	Yes	50%	75%	Yes	Yes
Skilled nursing facility care coinsurance	No	No	Yes	Yes	Yes	Yes	50%	75%	Yes	Yes
Part A deductible	No	Yes	Yes	Yes	Yes	Yes	50%	75%	50%	Yes
Part B deductible	No	No	Yes	No	Yes	No	No	No	No	No
Part B excess charge	No	No	No	No	Yes	Yes	No	No	No	No
Foreign travel exchange (up to plan limits)	No	No	80%	80%	80%	80%	No	No	80%	80%
Out-of-pocket limit	N/A	N/A	N/A	N/A	N/A	N/A	$4,960	$2,480	N/A	N/A

MEDICAID

Helping Those in Poverty

While Medicare is a program designed to help everyone in retirement with medical costs, Medicaid is aimed specifically at families with low incomes. It works in conjunction with the Children's Health Insurance Program (CHIP), which provides health insurance for children whose parents have low incomes but make too much money to qualify for Medicaid.

As of February 2016, 72.4 million people were enrolled in Medicaid and CHIP. Of these, approximately 35 million are children. There was a substantial increase in enrollment in these programs following the passage of the Affordable Care Act (Obamacare) in 2010.

WHERE DID IT COME FROM?

As has been previously mentioned, Medicaid, which debuted in 1965, was part of the Great Society social reforms instituted by the administration of President Lyndon Johnson.

The Great Society

In addition to strengthening Medicare and establishing Medicaid, the Great Society also included a number of important legislative initiatives. These included a series of civil rights acts that were designed to end systemic discrimination against African Americans; public education acts for providing financial aid to school districts across the country; and antipoverty acts.

The Medicaid program has been expanded several times over the years. For instance, in 1970 it began to cover people who were in intermediate care facilities. Since Medicaid is operated at the discretion of the state governments, it took some time for all the states to implement this benefit. In 1986, Medicaid assistance was extended to undocumented workers under certain circumstances.

In 1991 the Medicaid Drug Rebate Program began to help manage the cost of prescription drugs, and in 2000 the Breast and Cervical Cancer Treatment and Prevention Act covered any woman who has breast or cervical cancer.

After Obamacare passed in 2010, Medicaid began to offer a range of subsidies to help low-income people purchase health insurance. However, not all states are expanding subsidies in this way. (As of 2015, twenty-nine states plus Washington, D.C., have expanded Medicare. Twenty-one have decided not to do so.) To find out if your state is among those doing so, go to www.healthcare.gov/medicaid-chip/medicaid-expansion-and-you.

WHO QUALIFIES FOR MEDICAID BENEFITS?

Medicaid is a means-tested program, and eligibility is linked to poverty levels as determined by the federal government. However, there are other categories of people who may be eligible for Medicaid benefits. These beneficiaries include children from low-income families and low-income seniors. If you're enrolled for Supplementary Security Income (SSI), you're automatically enrolled in Medicaid.

Health Insurance Premium Payment Program (HIPP)

Some states operate a program called the Health Insurance Premium Payment Program. This program allows people to enroll in a private insurance program, which will be paid for by Medicaid. Rules and regulations vary from state to state.

Because Medicaid is administered at the state level, qualifications for it vary. But in general, you will be required to show your income in relation to the federal poverty level (FPL). The FPL changes from year to year to take inflation into account. Some states also take into account the assets you own, even if you're not using them at the moment. Assets can include such things as investments, goods (such as gold or jewelry), and money in savings accounts. Most states list several ways in which you can qualify for Medicaid.

In addition to the issue of your income, to be eligible for Medicaid in a particular state you must:

- Live in the state
- Be a U.S. citizen

Applying for Medicaid

Because of the state-by-state nature of Medicaid, you'll need to examine the specific requirements of the state in which you reside. You can find a list of contact addresses online at the Medicaid website: www.medicaid.gov/about-us/contact-us/contact-state-page .html. When applying, you'll need proof of citizenship. Appropriate documentation includes a U.S. passport, birth certificate, or other materials that identify you as a U.S. citizen. Visit the Medicaid website for details.

WHAT MEDICAID COVERS

Since Medicaid (unlike Medicare) assumes you have a very limited income, it covers a larger portion of medical expenses than does Medicare. Medicaid will:

- Pay for long-term nursing-home care
- Pay for glasses and hearing aids
- Pay out-of-pocket medical expenses (e.g., doctor's visit, physical therapy)
- Pay for more coverage than Medicare in long-term skilled nursing facilities

Children in Medicaid are eligible for comprehensive dental services, including maintenance and preventive measures. However, since many dentists don't participate in Medicaid, the number of people who actually use this service is limited.

SHIP

Need advice about Medicaid, Medicare, or any other aspect of government-run healthcare programs? Contact State Health Insurance Assistance Programs (SHIP). Counseling is free, and it's enormously helpful in navigating the rocks and rapids of healthcare. You can find out more about the program online at www.shiptacenter.org.

SPEND-DOWN PROGRAMS

It's possible that you make too much money to qualify for Medicaid. Nonetheless, you may still be able to receive Medicaid benefits. If you spend your excess income (that is, income above and beyond what the limit is for Medicaid in your state) on medical bills, that's called a spend-down, and it could mean you're qualified for Medicaid.

Four groups of people qualify for Medicaid spend-downs:

1. Children under twenty-one years of age
2. Blind or disabled people
3. Adults over sixty-five years of age
4. Families in which at least one of the parents is dead, disabled, or out of work

Just to be clear, qualifying for spend-down doesn't mean that Medicaid will pay *all* your medical expenses. You're responsible for paying medical bills from your excess amount. After that, Medicaid will pick up your medical expenses. It's sort of like an insurance deductible.

What Bills Count?
The following medical bills can count toward a spend-down:

- Your bills
- Your spouse's bills
- Your child's bills
- The bills for a child who isn't living with you but for whom you have financial responsibility
- Past unpaid medical bills (how much past will vary from state to state)

As well, you can count medical bills even if Medicaid doesn't cover them. However, bills for nonmedical services don't count.

If you are denied Medicaid, the Department of Social Services will send you a written notice telling you why your application has been rejected. It will also give you some information about the possibility of qualifying for a spend-down.

SOCIAL SECURITY AND YOUR RETIREMENT

Having a Rounded Financial Picture

As we remarked toward the beginning of this book, a very large number of people are situated so that they must rely entirely on Social Security to support them in retirement. This is a desolate picture, because unless you earned a great deal of money in your lifetime, your Social Security payments alone won't be large enough to provide you and your spouse with much of a retirement.

For 74 percent of single retirees and 52 percent of couples, Social Security represents more than half of their income. In 2009 it made up the sole source of income for 38 percent of people over sixty-five, and this number has certainly not declined since then. These figures, while not surprising, given the economic struggles of many people, are also somewhat disturbing, since Social Security wasn't designed to be anyone's only income in retirement. Rather, it was meant as a supplement to other income streams, helping older people to keep their heads above water and not sink into poverty. Social Security is an extremely important component of your retirement plan, but it's just that—one component.

However, there are some ways in which you can improve your financial situation, both before and after retirement. In doing your retirement planning, you can start by figuring out how to maximize your Social Security benefit. We've already discussed this in some detail. Here and in the next few sections, let's talk about some other sources of retirement income that can supplement your Social Security benefits.

SAVINGS

Remember the old story about the grasshopper and the ant? The thrifty, hard-working ant scrimped and saved and had a plentiful store of food for the winter. Meanwhile the careless grasshopper lived it up, but when the reckoning of winter came he had to beg for enough food to survive. Sadly, more of us are grasshoppers than ants. We tend not to begin saving until we're nearing retirement age. That said, some savings begun at *any* age is good. For many, distributions from their savings accounts won't replace Social Security benefits, but they can be very important supplements to them.

HAVE A PLAN

One of the principal reasons people struggle financially in retirement is that they don't start planning for it soon enough. When you're twenty-two and just beginning your working career, it may seem impossible to envision the day forty-five years or so later when you close the door to your workplace for the last time. But the sooner you can start to think about retirement, the more prepared you'll be for it when it happens.

To this end, there are several habits you can get into that will benefit you in anticipation of retirement:

- **Make and keep a budget.** When you're young, your budget will probably be fairly simple. But in all likelihood it will grow in complexity as you get older. Listing your income and your expenses gives you a very clear idea of whether or not you're living beyond your means. A budget will also help you to see what you can put aside in a savings account.

- **Decide what kind of retirement you want.** Many people, when they retire, remain exactly where they are and just stop going to work every morning. There's nothing wrong at all with such a plan. However, it's possible that you want to do something different: travel, move to another state (perhaps to be closer to your children or grandchildren), work part-time, go back to school, and so on. Each of these variations has different costs and different benefits. Do some research and find out what kind of retirement plan is right for you (a good place to start is Emily Guy Birken's book *Choose Your Retirement* as well as her book *The 5 Years Before You Retire*).
- **Take advantage of any employer-sponsored savings plans.** This applies particularly to 401(k) plans, and it's especially important if your employer matches your contribution. Such a contribution is really free money, and you should put yourself in a position to take full advantage of it. Find out the maximum amount your employer matches and contribute at least that percentage to your 401(k)—preferably more.
- **Set up your own savings plan.** Even a small amount put aside every week can mount up. Talk to your bank representative or other financial counselor about setting up an IRA. Discuss with them the advantages and disadvantages of a Roth IRA as opposed to a regular IRA.
- **Lead a frugal life.** Some books about retirement and savings will suggest things like giving up your weekly latte. This, in our opinion, is foolish. There's no point in making such tiny sacrifices if you're not looking at the bigger financial picture. We're not suggesting you enter a monastery or anything. All "frugal" means in this context is that you should avoid unnecessary spending.

There's nothing wrong with going to a nice restaurant for a good meal. But doing it every night is an expensive habit. It's great to go to the movies or take in a show. But do it every week and your budget will probably take a hit. "Everything in moderation" is a good philosophy to follow.

Social Security in the United Kingdom

Social Security in the UK, also called National Insurance, was first introduced in 1911. The post-war Labour government substantially expanded it, and despite significant blows during the Margaret Thatcher years, the system has survived to the present day. As of 2012–13, the government estimates that the fund paid out £91.012 billion and took in £84.263. Every child receives a National Insurance number prior to her or his sixteenth birthday. For purposes of contributions, employees are divided into a number of categories, and employers are responsible for determining which category applies to a particular employee.

KEEPING TRACK OF SOCIAL SECURITY

We've already talked about *my* Social Security (www.ssa.gov/my account). Once you open an account at this site, you can regularly view your statement and see how the size of your benefit grows as you work more and more years. Your statement will also indicate how many zeros you need to get rid of—remember, your top thirty-five years of income are used to average your primary insurance amount

(PIA), zeros included, so it's important to get them out of the way by working a full thirty-five years.

Make It a Family Decision

Since the issue of when to take your Social Security benefits is one that will affect your family, it's important to discuss it with them. Consider the issue of whether and when your spouse should take spousal benefits.

Your Expected Lifespan

No one really enjoys talking about her or his death, but it's important that you be realistic about your expected lifespan. The question of how long you can reasonably be expected to live has a big impact on the question of when to begin taking benefits. Consider such factors as heredity, your health history, and your personal habits, such as smoking and drinking.

DELAYING YOUR BENEFITS

As written many times in this book, in general your best strategy for Social Security is to delay taking benefits until you reach your full retirement age (FRA) and, if possible, until you reach age seventy. That's because your benefits will increase by 8 percent each year you delay taking them.

The problem, of course, is that it's very difficult for many people to go past age sixty-two without at least considering the option of starting their benefits. In some cases you may have been laid off from work and are struggling to find employment.

Age Discrimination

Title VII of the Civil Rights Act of 1964 makes it illegal to discriminate against someone because of their age. Unfortunately, this is a rule that's honored more in the breach than in the observance. Nonetheless, be aware that when you're interviewing for a job it's illegal for the interviewer to ask you your age. If the issue does come up, the best thing to do is stress your many years of experience and how valuable that experience can be to your potential employer.

Here are some things you should consider as you work to delay your benefits as long as possible.

- **Downsize.** As many people approach retirement, they find they can make do with a smaller house. A smaller house not only represents less of a physical challenge to maintain, it also means a smaller mortgage or rental payment. Downsizing also gives you an opportunity to declutter. Perhaps you've got children who are eager and willing to take some of the family furniture off your hands.

- **Move to another state.** Many lower-population states have lower costs of living as compared to higher population states (especially those in the Northeast). By moving to another state you may be able to substantially reduce your expenses.

- **Move to another country.** Many countries have substantially lower costs of living than the United States, especially those nations in Latin America. As noted earlier, you can continue receiving your Social Security benefits in many places abroad. And one tremendous asset in many—though not all—of these countries is that healthcare is socialized and therefore free or available at a greatly reduced cost. In some countries such as Panama, English is effectively the second language; in other countries English is widely spoken (although if you're going to live in another country, it would be good to learn the local language).

- **Find other sources of income.** These can range from teaching classes at your local community college (many colleges look for adjunct instructors with significant life experience) to offering your services online. Remember, the more sources of income you have, the less you'll need to rely solely on Social Security in retirement.
- **Create a retirement budget.** Get in the habit of budgeting at the beginning of your working life. A retirement budget will help you figure out what income you need in your golden years and where the money can come from. By the time you get close to your full retirement age, you'll know what your benefit from Social Security will be if you retire at your FRA, or what it will be if you wait to claim until you're older. Keep in mind that when you retire, certain expenses will go away. For instance, you won't have to spend money commuting to work. Nor will you be taking money from your paycheck to pay for a retirement account. And you won't be paying payroll taxes to help fund Social Security.

ENTERING RETIREMENT

As you enter your retirement, you should have, ideally, at least three sources of income:

1. Social Security
2. Savings, whether in the form of IRAs or a 401(k)
3. Work of some sort

These three income sources will help you achieve the kind of retirement you want.

Healthcare in Retirement

Healthcare expenses are likely to be your biggest budget item during your retirement. For this reason, it's a good idea, if possible, to remain on your employer's health plan as long as possible. If you're forced to go off the plan (for example, because your employer doesn't offer health benefits to retirees from the company), you have some options. Chief among these is COBRA, which stands for Consolidated Omnibus Reconciliation Act. COBRA gives you the option of continuing the same benefits you had when you were working, paid at the same rates as your employer. The downside: those rates are very high.

USING A FINANCIAL PLANNER

Bringing in the Experts

By this point you've probably realized that planning your retirement, especially the Social Security aspect of it, is hard work. You have to learn a great deal, and even if you are a quick study, sound advice for planning your retirement is not something you can just pull off the Internet and use uncritically. For these reasons, you may want to consult a financial planner.

ASK AN EXPERT

There are numerous advantages to talking to a retirement and/or financial planning expert:

- These people think about retirement planning for a living. They know the ins and outs of Social Security and how to plan for retirement, and they can be relied upon to give you their best advice.
- They're likely to know the latest changes in government rules and regulations about Social Security benefits, and how those changes might affect retirement planning.
- They can help you with a long-term plan for retirement so you don't stumble from financial crisis to financial crisis. Of course, it's up to you to actually carry out the plan, but a financial planner can help you see the road ahead.

WHO SHOULD I TALK TO?

There are plenty of financial advisors with websites; a lot of the sites are attractive and enticing. But you need to do a few things before you start contacting these service providers.

Decide What You Want

You can't ask anyone to do a job for you until you know what that job is. So sit down and decide what exactly you want your financial counselor to do for you. For example, do you want her to:

- Suggest investment opportunities?
- Advise you when to take Social Security benefits?
- Help set up a savings budget?
- Assist you with estate planning?

Social Security Questions

If you just have some questions about Social Security—how the system works or a specific question about your benefits—you probably don't need to go to the expense of hiring a financial advisor. You can contact the Social Security Administration at www.ssa.gov or call free at 1-800-772-1213. A representative of the SSA can take your call between 7 A.M. and 7 P.M. Monday through Friday. The SSA advises that phone waiting times are generally shorter in the middle of the week.

It will help to make a list of the questions and requests you have for a financial advisor.

Do Your Research

Hiring a financial advisor is a serious business; after all, you're entrusting her with your money, which means you're entrusting her with your prospects for a financially safe and happy retirement. This is your future on the line, so there's no need to rush into things. Take your time, and do your due diligence. Visit her website. See if she's been reviewed by Yelp or any other online review sites. Look at her qualifications. How long has she been in business? Does she say how many clients she's worked with? Has she worked with any businesses? Which ones? Are they ones you've heard of?

Be sure to get comfortable before you proceed. If you start to feel nervous, back off.

Many people are intimidated by the alphabet soup of initials that follow advisors' names. It's confusing, but the best thing is to hire someone who is a Certified Financial Planner (CFP). Many other titles require only minimal certification; too often they're there to impress unwary potential clients. Someone who is a CFP has taken a course, passed an exam, has had three years of experience as a financial planner, and has signed on to a code of ethics.

If you want to check up on your possible advisor's record, you can do so by contacting the Securities and Exchange Commission (SEC). Ask to see the advisor's Form ADV, which must be filed with the SEC. That will tell you whether the person has had any brushes with the law or regulatory bodies.

Ask about Licenses

Your financial advisor must hold a core Series 6 or 7 license but could also hold a 63, 64, or 65 Series license. Confirm that she holds one of these licenses before proceeding. If you have questions about the licenses your planner holds, you can contact the Financial

Industry Regulatory Authority (FINRA) for help. Their website is www.finra.org.

Ask about Payment

Before you begin doing business with your advisor, find out how much the services are going to cost, and how she expects to be paid. Some financial advisors are paid on a commission basis—that is, their fee is contingent on you purchasing a particular financial product. Others are paid a fee and a retainer. Both have advantages and disadvantages. In the case of a fee-based planner, they may charge you a percentage of your account, an hourly rate, or a flat fee for a consultation. Whatever the case, you need to know what this is going to cost you and then decide if it's worth it.

Look for Someone Well-Rounded

If the only thing your advisor knows about is estate planning, she's not going to be very helpful to you in negotiating the complicated maze of Social Security. You want someone who has a broad grasp of personal finance so that you too can make sense of it.

ESTABLISH A PLAN

At some point during the interview you conduct with your financial planner, ask her to show you some examples of work she's done for other clients, with their names blacked out. If these examples look satisfactory to you, ask her to sketch out a general retirement plan for you. She should be able to create one that includes income other than just Social Security. This may mean continuing to work in retirement (without, however, reaching an income level that triggers taxation of your benefits). Ultimately, her role is to help you establish an overall plan for retirement of which Social Security is a key component.

Registered Representatives

If you're interested in purchasing stocks or bonds, you will want to contact a registered representative (RR). These individuals are authorized to buy and sell securities, and they are licensed through FINRA (Financial Industry Regulatory Authority). They can offer you other financial services as well.

PLANNING FOR TOMORROW

Young People, Retirement, and Social Security

As we said at the beginning of this book, when you start your first full-time job Social Security and retirement are about the last things on your mind. After all, you've probably got around forty years before you even become eligible for Social Security, and a few years past that before reaching your full retirement age.

The truth is, you're never too young to start thinking about retirement. In fact these days, it's more important than ever to do that. Experience of the Great Recession of 2008–09 shows how easily nest eggs can be wiped out, almost overnight. On the other hand, a sound, long-term investing strategy can grow that nest egg if you start it when you're young. Compounding of earnings is so powerful that if you start investing in your twenties, you can amass a large sum with little effort by the time you are in your sixties or seventies. This removes the problem of figuring out how to live solely on Social Security for the remainder of your life, and it goes a long way toward ensuring a financially secure retirement. All that's required is a basic understanding of retirement plans and the commitment to start now.

THE YOUNGER, THE BETTER

If you're in your twenties or thirties, you may feel like you have all the time in the world to invest for retirement. Don't find out the hard way that you can't start in your forties and expect to catch up to those who started in their twenties. The younger you are when you start, the less you'll need to invest, thanks to the power of compounding and the length of time until retirement.

In the same way, don't wait until you turn sixty-two to start learning about the Social Security system. The earlier you study it and the more you know about it, the more you'll be able to anticipate the size of your benefit so that you can work to maximize it. You'll also be better prepared for unexpected events such as disability, the loss of a spouse, a child with disabilities, and so forth. The Social Security system, as we hope you appreciate by now, is incredibly complex and can take a long time to understand—not to mention that Congress may take it into its head to change elements of the system again before you reach your full retirement age.

Invest While You're Young

It's difficult to think ahead to your retirement when you're young. There are so many things you want to do and so little money at your disposal. Yet investing a relatively small amount of money in your twenties can save you from having to invest much more when you're in your forties and fifties such that you can live comfortably in retirement.

To illustrate, if you start contributing $750 a year (less than $15 a week) at the age of twenty-one and you earn 8 percent a year, at the age of sixty-five you'll have amassed $289,129. If you invest the same amount starting at age thirty, you'll have $139,577; and if you wait until age forty, you'll have only $59,216.

As we've made clear in this book, Social Security is not designed to be your sole source of retirement income. Fortunately you can participate in any number of plans designed to provide you with additional sources of income in retirement. Employers sponsor some of them; others are the do-it-yourself variety. Most employer-sponsored plans fall into one of three categories: defined benefit, defined contribution, and profit-sharing plans.

DEFINED-BENEFIT PLANS

Employer-sponsored defined-benefit plans, also known as pensions, provide a guaranteed income for the rest of your life after you retire. The amount varies depending on your years of service with the company, your salary, and your age at retirement. Your employer uses an actuarial formula to arrive at the amount to put into the fund each year to ensure there's enough to meet the future retirement needs of its employees. All funds are mingled in one account managed by your employer.

Vanishing Pension Plans

By the time you reach retirement age, traditional pension plans may be a thing of the past. They're already being replaced or supplemented in large numbers by defined-contribution plans, which put more of the responsibility for retirement savings on you and less on your employer. To give you an idea of the rate at which this is happening, in 1983, 175,000 companies had pension plans. By 2012 there were fewer than 44,000. That number has continued to drop, and some long-established pension plans (such as policemen, firemen, and teachers in Detroit and other troubled cities) are in danger of extinction.

DEFINED-CONTRIBUTION PLANS

Unlike defined-benefit plans, employee-sponsored defined-contribution plans don't guarantee a specific dollar amount at retirement. How much you receive depends on how much you and your employer contributed and how well your investments performed over the years. Your contributions, as well as the contributions made by your employer (if any), are always kept in an individual account in your name.

With defined-contribution plans, you're in the driver's seat when it comes to deciding how your money will be invested. You'll choose from a variety of stock or bond mutual funds, guaranteed funds, annuities, cash equivalents like money market accounts, and your company's stock. Your plan will stipulate how frequently you can change your investment choices. Many plans allow you to manage your account online and make investment changes as often as you like.

One of the attractive features of defined-contribution plans is that they're portable. If you change jobs, you can take your money with you. We've talked about some of these a bit already (mainly the 401(k)), but here's a recap of the most common defined-contribution plans:

- 401(k) plans, offered by private companies
- 403(b) plans, offered by nonprofit, tax-exempt employers, such as schools and colleges, hospitals, museums, and foundations
- 457 plans, offered by federal, state, and local government agencies and nonprofit organizations

Other defined-contribution plans include Employee Stock Ownership Plans (ESOPs), money purchase plans, profit-sharing plans, simplified employee pension (SEP) plans, savings incentive match plans for employees (SIMPLEs), and Thrift Savings Plans (TSPs). These plans all have one important thing in common: You pay no taxes on your contributions or your earnings until you withdraw the money.

401(K) PLANS

One of the best things Congress ever did was create the 401(k) plan, an employer-sponsored retirement plan that gives a special tax break to employees saving for retirement. Here's how the tax break works: If, for example, you contribute $2,000 a year and you're in the 28 percent federal tax bracket, you'll save $560 because the $2,000 is deducted from your pay before your taxes are calculated. If you live in one of the states where 401(k) contributions are tax-deferred, and you're in a 6 percent state income tax bracket, you'll save another $120 in state taxes, for a total savings of $680.

The bottom line is that you add $2,000 to your investment account but only $1,320 comes out of your pocket ($2,000 − $680 = $1,320). It's like getting a raise. You don't pay taxes on your earnings until you withdraw them, presumably at retirement, so your investments grow faster as your untaxed earnings benefit from compounding.

Employer Match

To sweeten the pot even more, many employers match a certain percentage of your contributions. The amounts vary but a typical match is between fifty cents and $1 for every dollar you contribute, up to 6 percent of your salary. Even if your employer doesn't contribute, 401(k) plans are great, but if a match is offered and you don't participate, it's like walking past money lying on the sidewalk and not picking it up. Where else are you going to find a guaranteed 100 percent return on your money (assuming your employer matches dollar for dollar)? Actually, the return is greater than 100 percent when you factor in your tax savings.

Contribution Limits

The IRS sets limits, adjusted annually for inflation, on how much you can contribute to a 401(k) plan each year. As of 2015, the limit was $18,000 as long as it doesn't exceed 25 percent of your combined wages and your employer's contributions. The total of all contributions, including yours and your employer's, cannot exceed 100 percent of your compensation for the year, or $53,000, whichever is less.

Your employer is subject to strict IRS regulations to ensure that your 401(k) plan doesn't discriminate against lower-paid employees. If you're a highly compensated employee, your contributions will be limited by how much the less highly compensated employees contribute. Highly compensated employees are defined as those who made $110,000 per year and were among the top 20 percent earners in the company. Your employer may have adopted a safe harbor provision that does away with the limits for highly compensated employees by making a certain level of matching contributions or nonelective employer contributions for all eligible employees. To find out the rules of your plan, talk to a representative of the human resources department or to the plan's administrator.

401(k) Vesting

You're always 100 percent vested in your own contributions to the plan. The employer match is often subject to vesting, which means you earn the right to it gradually, over a number of years of employment with the company. There are two types of vesting schedules. About half of all 401(k) plans have cliff vesting, where you don't own any of the matching contributions until you've worked for the company for a certain amount of time. The Tax Relief Reconciliation Act of 2001 shortened the maximum vesting schedule for cliff vesting to no more than three years. The other type of vesting schedule is graded vesting, where you own an increasing percentage of the employer match over several years. Under the Pension Protection Act of 2006, vesting must take place in no more than six years. A typical vesting schedule is 20 percent after the second year, 40 percent after the third year, 60 percent after the fourth year, 80 percent after the fifth year, and 100 percent after the sixth year.

Don't Leave Money on the Table

If you earn $30,000 and your employer matches 100 percent of your 401(k) contributions up to 6 percent of your salary, you'd have to contribute $1,800 per year ($30,000 × 0.06 = $1,800) to take full advantage of the employer match. Any less than that and you'd be leaving money on the table.

It's important to consider the impact on your 401(k) when you're thinking of changing jobs. If your plan has cliff vesting, and you leave before working the required number of years, you walk away from everything your employer has contributed as matching funds, which could be a substantial amount. You could possibly earn thousands of additional dollars in company matching funds by staying in your current job for a few more months or years. Let's assume you had matching contributions of $6,000 and a vesting schedule of 20 percent per year for five years. If you left for a new job after three years, you'd take $3,600 ($6,000 × 60 percent = $3,600) of matching funds with you, plus all the contributions you made from your salary and any associated earnings.

Good deal, right? Yes, but it could be better if you stayed longer. Leaving after the three years means you'll forfeit $2,400 ($6,000 × 40 percent = $2,400) plus any earnings that money has accumulated. You could miss a whole year's worth of vesting by leaving a month or week before your vesting date.

Switching Jobs

The portability of 401(k) plans is a great feature, but what do you do with your money when you change jobs? You have three choices:

1. If you have over $5,000 in your account, you have the option of leaving your funds in your employer's plan.
2. You may be able to roll your balance over into your new employer's plan.
3. You can set up an individual IRA at a bank, through a broker, or directly with a mutual fund.

401(k) Loans

If your 401(k) plan allows loans, you can borrow up to 50 percent of your vested balance, not to exceed $50,000. Loans typically have to be repaid over no more than five years unless the funds are used to buy a first home. Interest rates are typically low—between one and three points above the prime rate. Because you pay yourself back instead of paying a creditor, 401(k) loans are touted as a great deal. Even the interest you pay goes back into your 401(k).

But it's not as simple as it sounds. The first reason you should avoid borrowing from your 401(k) if possible is the tax consequences. Your repayments are not tax-sheltered. They're made with after-tax money. If your monthly payment is $200 and you're in the 28 percent federal tax bracket and a 6 percent state tax bracket, you'd have to make $303 to net enough to make the payment. Worse, when you retire and take withdrawals, you pay taxes on that money again. The second reason you shouldn't borrow from your 401(k) is the opportunity costs. The money that you borrow could be earning interest or appreciating if you left it in your plan. Over time, the impact on your 401(k) could be substantial.

401(k) Loan Statistics

According to a report on the business and finance website CNNMoney, at the end of 2014 the average 401(k) account balance, net of loans, was a record $91,300, a leap of 30 percent from 2011. Workers and employers contributed an average of $9,160 to the plans in 2014.

If you have a loan balance when you leave your job, you'll be required to repay the loan immediately. If you don't, you'll owe federal and state income taxes on the amount you borrowed, plus a 10 percent early withdrawal penalty. Think carefully before borrowing your retirement funds, and do so only if you need the money for something important, like a down payment on a house, and you have no other alternatives. Never borrow from your 401(k) for something like a vacation or a new car.

403(B) AND 457 PLANS

403(b) plans are defined-contribution plans used by nonprofit organizations. They work very much like 401(k) plans. Your contributions are tax-deductible and your earnings are tax-deferred until you take the money out at retirement. Like 401(k) plans, the amounts that you and your employer can contribute are limited by law.

Section 457 plans are defined-contribution plans established by government agencies. Like 401(k) and 403(b) plans, they allow you to make tax-deductible contributions and your earnings grow tax-deferred until retirement. One important difference is that your account is funded solely by your own contributions. Your employer doesn't contribute a dime. These plans are still a great benefit because of their tax-deferred feature, but not as great as a 401(k), 403(b), or other plans that include an employer match.

INDIVIDUAL RETIREMENT ACCOUNTS

We've talked a bit about these accounts before, but now it's time to go into them in more depth so you can see how they form an important supplement to your Social Security benefits in retirement planning.

Individual retirement accounts or IRAs have evolved in the more than forty years since they were established, and they now include such variations as SEP IRAs, Roth IRAs, SIMPLE IRAs, and more. IRAs provide the same tax-deferred benefits as 401(k) and similar employer-sponsored plans and allow you to decide how your funds will be invested.

If you have employment income, you can contribute up to $5,500 a year to an IRA ($6,500 if you're aged fifty or more). This figure includes *all* the money you contribute annually to *all* your IRAs, whether they're traditional, Roth, and so on. You can set up an IRA through most banks and financial institutions, or through a mutual fund company or broker. You can start making withdrawals at age fifty-nine and a half, and you must start doing so by age seventy and a half. Like 401(k) plans, a 10 percent penalty is placed on any funds you take out early unless you retire, need the money to pay medical expenses, or are disabled.

Contributing to an IRA doesn't make sense unless you're maximizing your contributions to your 401(k) or 403(b) plan by contributing the IRS limit. Take full advantage of these employer-sponsored defined-contribution plans first and if you have money left to invest for retirement, consider IRAs. If you don't have access to an employer-sponsored plan, then by all means, invest as much as possible in IRAs.

Online Calculators

Use the online calculators at Charles Schwab to help you determine which IRA you're eligible for and whether you should convert your IRA to a Roth IRA.

Traditional IRAs

If you are filing taxes as an individual and your annual income is less than $61,000, you can deduct all of your IRA contributions up to the contribution limit. If your income is between $61,000 and $71,000, you can deduct some of your IRA contributions. If you make more than $71,000, you can't take this deduction. (If you file as a married couple, your range is $98,000 to $118,000.) You have until April 15 to make an IRA contribution for the previous year, but make sure to do it before filing your income taxes. The IRS will check to make sure your contribution was made within the deadline.

Roth IRAs

There are several important distinctions between traditional IRAs and Roth IRAs. Traditional IRA contributions are tax-deductible. Roth IRA contributions are not. Traditional IRAs grow tax-deferred until you withdraw the funds at retirement, and then they're taxed at your regular income tax rate. Roth IRAs earnings are never taxed. You're required to withdraw a minimum amount each year from your traditional IRAs once you reach the age of seventy and a half. There are no such requirements for Roth IRAs.

SIMPLE IRAs and SEPs

The savings incentive match plan for employees (SIMPLE) IRA is a plan offered by businesses with no other retirement plans and with fewer than 100 employees. As in 401(k) plans, your contributions and earnings are tax-deferred. You can contribute up to $12,500 a year, and your employer must either match 100 percent of your contributions, up to 3 percent of your salary, or contribute 2 percent of compensation (up to $5,300) for each eligible employee, even those who don't contribute to the plan.

A simplified employee pension (SEP) IRA is similar to a SIMPLE IRA, except that only your employer can contribute. The disadvantage of this plan is that you have no control over how much goes into your plan because you can't contribute any of your own money unless you're self-employed and contribute your own money. The limit on employer contributions is 15 percent of your compensation up to a maximum of $40,000. With both the SIMPLE IRAs and the SEP IRAs, you can still invest in a traditional or Roth IRA.

Choosing the Best IRA for You

It can be difficult to determine whether you'd come out ahead in the long run with a traditional or a Roth IRA. It depends on a number of factors, such as how long before you retire, when you plan to start taking money out, and your tax bracket now and at retirement. There are benefits to Roth IRAs besides tax-free earnings. In some cases you can withdraw your contributions before retirement without owing taxes or penalties, although you may have to pay taxes on the withdrawal. You can withdraw up to $10,000 in earnings without penalty to buy your first home if the money has been in the Roth IRA for at least five tax years, to pay medical expenses exceeding 7.5 percent of your gross income, to pay college expenses for certain family members, or to use if you're unable to work because of disability. Any other withdrawals before the age of fifty-nine and a half will be subject to the penalty.

If You Make Too Much Money

If your income exceeds the limits for a traditional IRA, you can still contribute but it won't be tax-deductible. Since tax-deductibility is the biggest advantage of a traditional IRA, if you don't qualify for the tax deduction, then a Roth IRA is probably the best choice.

KEOGH PLANS

Keoghs are tax-deferred retirement plans for people who have self-employment income. The IRS no longer uses the term "Keogh plan," but two types of defined-contribution plans are still referred to as Keoghs by most people: profit sharing and money purchase plans.

Money purchase Keoghs require the same contribution each year even if you don't make a profit. Contributions are limited to the lesser of $52,000 or 25 percent of your self-employment income. Contributions to profit-sharing Keoghs can be zero to 25 percent of self-employment income up to $40,000 and can change each year. These are complex plans and will require the services of an accountant or other professional to establish.

CHOOSING THE RIGHT INVESTMENTS

If you have a traditional pension plan, your employer makes all the investment decisions for you. With most of the other retirement plans discussed in this chapter, you're in the driver's seat. Some people find that intimidating, but it doesn't have to be. Various investment options are probably available in your retirement plan: stocks, bonds, mutual funds, cash equivalents, and maybe your employer's stock. Putting all your funds in one type of investment increases your risk of loss if that investment doesn't perform well, so spread your funds out over several types of investments.

Stocks, Bonds, and Mutual Funds

With retirement investing, it's important to think long-term. Because retirement earnings grow tax-deferred and you have many years before you'll make withdrawals, retirement plans are best suited for your most aggressive investing, which means stocks and mutual funds. Don't make the mistake of putting all your money in money market funds or guaranteed investment contracts (GICs). Diversify your portfolio to balance risk and reward, and you should come out far ahead in the long-term. This doesn't mean you shouldn't choose your investments carefully. If 80 percent of your retirement funds are in stock mutual funds, most of it should be in well-established funds with a history of solid performance. If you want to get aggressive with some of your money, you can place a small percentage of your stock investments in higher-risk funds.

ESOPs

Again, we stress, don't put all your eggs in one basket. Thousands of employees who did so lost their entire retirement funds when their employer's stock lost value due to corruption or shaky accounting practices that hid serious financial problems. If company stock is the only option available to you in your 401(k) plan, look at other investment vehicles for some of your retirement savings.

Annuities

When you buy an annuity, you sign a contract with an insurance company that stipulates the amount of your investment, whether you choose a fixed or variable rate for interest, the method of payment, and any fees. Fixed-rate annuities guarantee a specific interest rate for the life of the annuity. Interest rates on variable-rate annuities fluctuate with the ups and downs of the financial markets. You can invest with one lump-sum payment or build it gradually over time.

Your earnings grow tax-deferred, but the money you put in is not tax-deductible, so this is an investment best suited for someone who has taken full advantage of all the tax-deductible plans available and still has money left over to invest. It's unlikely that the average person in her or his twenties or thirties would choose this investment vehicle, but you should be aware of it in case an insurance agent attempts to sell you one.

THINK ABOUT YOUR SOCIAL SECURITY FUTURE

Even though the day when you file for your Social Security benefits may be far in the future, you should give some thought to it now. Open a *my* Social Security account (www.ssa.gov/myaccount) and regularly check your statement. Watch as your annual earnings gradually replace those zeros and the size of your benefit grows. Think about what you want to do in retirement and how your Social Security benefits can help you. Be familiar with spousal benefits and disability benefits as well as things such as children with disability benefits. Life throws a lot of curve balls at us, and the more prepared we are for them, the better our chances of knocking them out of the park.

If you plan ahead, strive to constantly increase your knowledge, and multiply possible income streams, there's every reason for you to be confident in a long, financially secure retirement.

FINDING HAPPINESS IN RETIREMENT

Will Your Retirement Be an Ending or a Beginning?

Up to this point we've been talking in great detail about the mechanics of Social Security. But we need to keep in mind that Social Security is, after all, a means to an end. That end, for most beneficiaries, is a financially secure retirement. At the same time, in an age where life expectancy is increasing, retirees are finding new challenges to their retirement years. In the next few sections we'll look at some of those challenges and how to meet them with the aid of Social Security and other means.

The dictionary defines "retire" with depressing phrases such as "withdraw from the world," "disappear from sight," "seek seclusion or shelter," or even "go to bed." That may have been your father's, or your grandfather's, way to retire, but will it be yours? Not necessarily. The current generation is actively pursuing hobbies and business ventures into retirement.

WHAT TO CALL IT

For the better part of the past century, American society, with government and employer support, has been organized to "take care" of its vulnerable citizens—the very young and the elderly—who cannot care for themselves. Throughout history, people have worked until they were no longer able. In traditional societies, family units are comprised of succeeding generations—babies, parents, grandparents, maybe even great-grandparents, cousins, uncles, and aunts—where the very youngest and the oldest are cared for by more able family members. You can think of this as a family-based system of social security. This is definitely not the retirement system that we modern Americans know today.

Social Security currently considers full retirement age to be sixty-seven. This is, in effect, the age that our government says you can stop work voluntarily. Minus a tragic illness or major disability, reaching full retirement age doesn't necessarily mean you can't work. In fact, many seniors hope to push that retirement age back another five or ten years. Indeed, when you look around at people you know who are sixty-seven, do you see withered-up, apathetic, no-more-juice individuals? Or do you see people who match the images seen in the financial services ads portraying adults who have a lot of energy and zest for life? Somehow the notion of rocking away the years of retirement no longer jibes with how people see others or themselves.

High Mental Functioning

A ten-year MacArthur Foundation study of people age seventy to eighty showed that those with the highest mental functioning had three traits in common: They were more mentally active, more physically active, and had a sense of their contribution to the world around them. The key to having the highest mental functioning is having all three traits, not just one.

There is a growing trend toward redefining the stage of adulthood between middle age and really old age. There are many commonly used terms to define this period of life that no longer seem to fit well:

- Golden years
- Mature

- Old age
- Aged
- The elderly
- Life of leisure
- Retirement

Evolving terms associated with retirement years include:

- Third-agers
- My time
- Social entrepreneurship
- Second adolescence

Nancy Schlossberg calls this period "my time" because it follows the conclusion of major earlier adult responsibilities, such as raising children or holding down a job for thirty years or more. At this stage in life, personal interests and goals can be pursued unimpeded. Marc Freedman, head of Encore.org (formerly Civic Ventures) based in San Francisco and author of *The Big Shift: Navigating the New Stage Beyond Midlife*, offers a fresh view of what it means to be an older adult in America. He suggests that when you are living in the third age, the things most important to you will be:

- Lifelong learning
- Finding new ways to contribute to society
- Continued physical and spiritual well-being
- Being in a community of people who share the same goals
- Finding places to get resources for figuring out this stage of life

The senior centers that are organized to fill the hours of the bored and lonely with bingo games and shuffleboard no longer fill the bill. Don't think you need to sit on the sidelines while this new social dynamic unfolds. You can be front and center. Your body can be stronger at sixty than your father's was at sixty. Your mind can be sharper at eighty than your mother's was at eighty.

Social Security in Spain

Spain has one of the world's older systems of social welfare, dating back to 1883. It is now enshrined in the Spanish constitution, drafted and passed in 1978 after the fall of Francisco Franco. The system provides benefits for:

- Healthcare
- Medical care in case of illness or accident
- Maternity
- Death and survival
- Retirement
- Disability

Employers' contributions are substantially larger than those of employees. For example, for unemployment benefits the employee contributes 1.55 percent, while the employer contributes 5.5 percent.

As you move away from the full-time paid workforce, you can have a role shaping the institutions and services designed to help you have a happy and fulfilling third age. Some terrific work has already begun, but it will be up to you and your peers to take it to the next level. Meanwhile, new terminology will continue to pop up in the culture that tries to capture what the new retirement means.

YOUR DREAM RETIREMENT

Options for Ending Work

Do you have your own dream retirement worked out in your mind yet? Have you thought about how long you will be in retirement? Do you think you'll be doing the same activities in your eighties that you did in your sixties? If you are a forty-year-old reading this, statistically you have only lived half of your life. Do you plan to be in the employ of only one company by the time you decide to finally call it quits, or do you imagine traversing through a variety of career moves on a zigzag approach to your third age?

You may think you are far too busy with your current obligations to spend any amount of mental energy to forecast goals for what you will be doing in your fifties, sixties, seventies, eighties, and beyond. But the truth is, no matter the plans you make or the paths you take, with the aid of some thoughtful preparation you can embrace the ambiguity of your own post-work life and make it a good thing, not a paralyzing event.

Some scenarios for moving through the latter stages of your career include:

- **Winding down, but not out.** Would your employer permit you to move from a full-time work schedule to a part-time one?
- **Making a trial run.** How about taking a solid month off from work to test drive being home 24/7? If someone else is in the house, will you be able to accommodate each other?
- **Deciding to change directions.** Do you have an entrepreneurial itch that has never been scratched? Ready to leave the factory and open a card store?

- **Redirecting your commitments.** Maybe you need a much-deserved rest, but could you envision taking on new responsibilities? More than likely, the board of a charity you care about in your community will welcome you with open arms.
- **Exploring your talents.** Is there an interest or skill you have been postponing developing because you simply didn't have time? Ready to audition for the community improv troupe or learn another language?
- **Engaging in the new.** Maybe you want to travel, but you cannot imagine idling away your days at a beach resort. As it so happens, there are many programs that encourage you to learn and contribute while seeing something new.

So many uncharted paths are awaiting you. The key to success will be how well you cope with the changes you experience.

Challenges to a Part-Time Schedule

Easing into retirement by cutting your full-time work schedule to part-time can be tricky. You may be able to afford a reduced paycheck, but your coworkers may be unable to honor your part-time status. As a result, you may end up becoming a part-time volunteer.

It is a worthwhile exercise to observe others who are ahead of you on the path to their third age. Watch them and ask them what is working and what they would change if they could.

IF A DOOR CLOSES

Look for the Open Window

Sometimes retirement planning gets short-circuited. The technology company you began working for when you were in your late thirties grew and grew. Twenty years later it was bought by a bigger firm. You had stock options that were the major bulk of your retirement game plan until a dizzying downturn in the economy essentially vaporized not only your stock but the company itself, leaving you with ashes in your retirement account. Now what? This was not the scenario you had envisioned as you put in those twelve-hour days and traveled for your employer over weekends, all with a goal of building something great and realizing a juicy payoff at some point.

Dealing with a Career Setback

A career setback has to be viewed as just that—a setback. It does not mean you will never earn money again, or that you will never be able to retire. What you need to hold on to is your sense of self-worth and a realistic view of your skills, experience, and talents.

FLEXIBILITY IS KEY

The answer for this, or any radical change in your career path, is to remain flexible. Sure, the prospect of seeing your life savings wiped out is a legitimate reason for angst, grief, and anger. But you cannot stay in the valley of self-pity for long, because you need to pick yourself up and get going again. If you are going to find a new stream of income, you can do one of two things: Find someone to hire you or hire yourself.

Your first instinct upon losing a job could be to hurry up and find another that will put you right back on the track you left with similar responsibilities, perks, and pay. As well, of course, you will want to avoid having any of those zero-earning years that are, during your retirement, going to affect the size of your Social Security benefit.

The problem is that finding another job immediately may not be possible. If you lost your job as a result of an industry meltdown, there may not be jobs for your exact experience at the moment. You might have to think long and hard about making a major career twist, one that will carry you into and through the third age you may be approaching chronologically. This could be an opportunity to launch yourself into entirely new and exciting opportunities. Perhaps you should:

- Slow down the pace.
- Convert a hobby or favorite pastime into a business.
- Drop everything and move somewhere you'd prefer living.
- Take a year off and sail around the world.

Depending on your age, and what other financial resources you have salted away at the time of a career interruption, your choices can be either wide open or driven by a need to rebuild savings and earn a reliable income.

If you encounter a career blowup when you are at an age that makes you less attractive in the marketplace (it may be ageist, but the older you are the harder it is to get hired for top jobs), you can figure out ways to repackage what you have to offer. You might have received the boot from a retailer, but your experience may be of keen interest to a market-research firm. Instead of working a predictable Monday to Friday schedule with set hours, you can reshape your work time into billable hours as a consultant. Don't be surprised to find you actually prefer this autonomy. Besides current income, it can carry you for many years into what would have formerly been considered leisure retirement years. All of a sudden the panic associated with job loss late in the game is replaced with an understanding that, as the rules loosen for how and when people retire, the risks associated with not having every duck in order at some arbitrary age are reduced.

Starting a Small Business

Many people who have lost their jobs consider starting small businesses. This can be a great plan, but it's not something you should rush into. Before starting a small business, do some research, draw up a detailed business plan, and above all, make sure you've got sufficient savings to support you while the business ramps up. Melinda Emerson, author of *Become Your Own Boss in 12 Months*, suggests that you, as a prospective entrepreneur, should have "enough money to support yourself or your family for a year or two, along with a year's worth of working capital."

BEING A FORWARD-THINKING RETIREE

People all across the spectrum are experiencing a new way of defining what the later years of life should be like. One high-profile example is John Glenn, whose early career shot him into space in manned space missions. After retiring from the military and flying into space, Mr. Glenn ran for public office and served in the U.S. Senate for the state of Ohio. Of all his contributions to society, he may best be remembered for his decision to apply for permission to train for, and join, the crew of a space flight in his seventies. He is quoted as saying, "Just because you're up in years some doesn't mean you don't have hopes and dreams and aspirations just as much as younger people do."

Consider Retraining

If you experience a work setback, you should take a good look at your qualities as a member of the workforce. As you contemplate a new work direction, you may need to take a self-inventory of what kind of training or education would make you a more attractive employee—or give you the tools to start your own business. Even if you've reached retirement age and elect to begin taking your Social Security benefits, retraining can open up possibilities for creating new streams of income in retirement—something that's very desirable.

Other examples of older people continuing to contribute to society despite being the age of most retirees are at least three past U.S. presidents. Bill Clinton and George H.W. Bush teamed up at the request of President George W. Bush to lead a worldwide relief and rebuilding effort for the areas devastated by a tsunami in South Asia. Jimmy Carter, who left office in 1980, went on to create The Atlanta Project (TAP), bringing rich and poor together to serve the community as a whole. He probably single-handedly put Habitat for Humanity on the map by donning a work apron and grabbing a hammer and nails. He and his wife, Rosalynn, established the Carter Center. He became a diplomat "without portfolio," stepping into some of the stickiest political wickets on the planet, and was able to bring warring parties to peaceful compromise, earning himself the Nobel Peace Prize along the way.

If President Carter felt he had left office with a job unfinished, he found new spheres in which to express his many talents. In the process he has, with his wife, shared his experience of reinventing himself later in life by authoring two books: *Everything to Gain: Making the Most of the Rest of Your Life* and *The Virtues of Aging*. His view may best be summed up with his quote: "Retirement has not been the end but a new beginning."

THE NEW RETIREMENT

No Rocking Chairs for Baby Boomers

When it comes to retirement these days, tear up the script and throw out the rule book. Old age never looked so good. One thing about baby boomers, they never saw a mold they didn't want to break. A lifetime of rewriting the script for how life should be lived is not going to end with retirement. The values that are important to baby boomers will carry through every decade of their lives and will change the way the generations that follow think of retirement.

THE BOOMER PHILOSOPHY

The same spirit of rugged individualism that launched settlers across frigid plains in the nineteenth century, and astronauts into outer space in the twentieth, is fully ingrained in the American psyche. That powerful combination of optimism and drive has been embraced by the boomer generation (born between 1946 and 1964) as they leave behind their careers. If you are among those at the early end of this demographic, you are already leading the charge to redefining the options for life after work. Those following close on your heels will be piggybacking on your initiatives, bringing more imagination and creativity to leading healthy, fulfilling, and well-balanced lives in their fifties, sixties, and beyond.

Boomers might want a respite from hard-charging careers, but it won't be long before they trade in their trader desks for tracking global warming trends in their newfound free time.

PLAN FOR INCOME, PLAN FOR LIVING

To successfully retire it takes discipline and diligent management of savings and investments. You must stitch together the income sources needed to carry you for perhaps decades. One of the key lessons we hope you've learned is that Social Security is an important— perhaps *the* most important—element in your financial planning for retirement. You should remain doggedly committed to "paying yourself" every pay period and, most importantly, not give in to the temptation to spend any monies if they pass through your hands in transition from one retirement plan to another. Simply put, you need to turn time to your advantage. And you do this by putting money into retirement accounts right from the start of your working days and leaving them there to grow.

You should look to maximize your Social Security benefit by not beginning your benefits until you reach your full retirement age or, if possible, until age seventy. You should also be aware of other Social Security strategies and issues, such as the retroactive lump-sum provision and the Windfall Elimination Provision.

All of these things contribute to your retirement success, which is the overall goal here.

BUDGET

The best way to plan for retirement is to draw up a budget. The kind of budget you create will depend very much on what kind of retirement you want to have. (For an outline of various retirement options and their probable costs, see Emily Guy Birken, *Choose Your Retirement*.)

In one column put your projected monthly Social Security benefit (we'll discuss how to arrive at this number shortly). Then add revenue from your other projected income streams. These can include annual distributions from your 401(k) and IRA, divided by twelve; money from any freelance work you plan to do in retirement; annuities; investment income—anything to put on the plus side of the ledger.

In the second column, make a comprehensive list of monthly expenses: rent or mortgage, gas, food, utilities, credit card bills, and so on.

In this way, you can get a clearer picture not only of whether your retirement as you envision it is financially feasible but what sort of role Social Security plays in it. Social Security is important, there's no question. But when it comes to a financially secure retirement, it shouldn't be your only reliable source of income.

Life Planning

As we've said, the old norms for defining retirement are eroding—the exciting evolution under way is bringing new life to what had been considered the quiet years of old age. You will be blessed with the time and hopefully the energy to pursue in your interests during your post-work years. Consequently, you will need to do some long-term planning for how you will live in retirement. Just as with financial planning, life planning requires thoughtful deliberation of options. Before you can pick from the choices that appeal to you, you should do some research to learn more about your areas of interest. These can cover a range of possibilities and may include:

- Traveling—exotic, social-service oriented, environmental, luxurious, or rugged
- Developing nascent interests
- Volunteering in your community, or across the globe
- Taking classes to learn new skills
- Working on political issues
- Being a mentor
- Becoming more connected to neighbors
- Organizing socials

When you are deep in the trenches of your workaday life you may be so busy that you can barely claw your way through the daily demands of your job and personal life, much less find the time to explore dimensions of how you will live your life later. Yet before you know it, your friends are building a little vacation house with a view toward moving there full-time for their retirement; you realize that your kids are able to drive themselves to their many activities; and you are nearing the number of years worked at your firm to become fully vested in the retirement plan. Suddenly it is time to take the long view ahead. You should look across the decades, not just at next month's calendar that is already jammed with commitments. As you take in the long view, start sketching out a vision of the following dimensions of your life:

- Housing options for each decade after fifty
- "Down time" you'll need daily and weekly, and what form it might take
- Activities for relaxation, stimulation, or escape
- Components of a healthy lifestyle

- Social life
- Spiritual life
- Family obligations

It is no secret that the expectations for job performance have ramped up to red zone levels of intensity for many people. With instant access to information online, the ease of shooting messages back and forth via e-mail and text messaging, and the demands of social media, cultural norms for communication have shifted to put intense emphasis on speed. Taking time to weigh options, reflecting upon a response before firing it off, or having the time to gather all relevant information to formulate a considered solution to a problem is becoming as archaic as the Ford Model T.

If you are going to do a good job of getting your mind, as well as your wallet, prepared for retirement, you somehow will need to find a way to carve out time and space for reflecting upon, and planning for, how you expect your transition out of work to go. Jeri Sedlar and Rick Miners wrote a book together called *Don't Retire, Rewire!* In it they offer the following list of questions to ask yourself as a start for discovering what shape your retirement might take:

1. What picture comes to mind when you imagine being retired?
2. What do you anticipate adding to your life in retirement?
3. What do you picture giving up?
4. Do you have ideas for what your retirement should be?
5. How about not retiring? What image comes to mind? Something positive? Something negative?
6. Have you observed retirements of friends? Parents? Relatives?
7. What parts of what you have seen would you emulate, or do differently?

Counsel for Financial and Life Planning

Earlier we talked about what you should do to select a financial planning advisor to help you cope with Social Security and overall retirement planning. In much the same way you can seek counsel for the life planning part of your coming decades.

As a reminder, your financial planning advisor may ask you to articulate the concrete needs of your retirement:

- Will you be able to live where you are now? For how long?
- How will your healthcare needs be met?
- Do you need tax planning for your estate?
- What will be your income sources?

He will then help you find the way to put the dollars together for those goals. This financial expert may not have the skills to tease out the more esoteric dimensions of thinking through what shape your retirement might take. For that, you will need to do some life planning. Some resources to help you develop a retirement *life* plan are:

- Use a life coach.
- Keep a journal of your dreams, goals, and desires.
- Read books and articles.
- Follow trends in all media, including movies and TV. Observe how older people are portrayed—cranky and passive, or vibrant and useful? Do you see yourself in these images?
- Talk to people you know who have experience in retirement, including those who may have come out of retirement and returned to work.

You can find many websites that address dimensions of retirement other than those that are exclusively financial. A few examples are:

- http://retiredamericans.org
- www.aarp.com
- www.forbes.com/forbes
- http://money.usnews.com/money/retirement

Creating a retirement life plan will be an ongoing process, continuing even once you are in retirement. The more effort you put into preparing yourself by declaring your dreams and expectations (even if only in the privacy of a journal), the more likely you will come up with a game plan you can follow.

When Two Are Involved

If you have a spouse or partner, you will need to create both individual life plans and a team plan. If you do not expect to be retiring around the same time, there may be some significant juggling of goals and expectations, or at least defining their timelines. Some instances in which couples may be out of sync with their retirement launches are:

- When there is an age spread of ten or more years
- When one partner has had a later start getting into a particular retirement plan (in a school system, for instance) and needs to put in the requisite years to reap the benefits
- When a stay-at-home spouse takes on employment around the same time the other spouse gets ready to sell a business and get out of the workaday world

- When one partner needs to stop working due to a serious health problem or disability

It is hard enough trying to get your own life sorted out, and it is all that much harder to manage the complexity of creating workable plans for two people. This is all the more reason you really must treat the life-planning facet of your retirement with the same care and seriousness you apply to financial preparedness.

Go for the Discount

Don't be shy about grabbing every possible senior discount you can. From movie tickets to car washes, you can find ways to save. Some of the biggest retailers offer senior discounts on a midweek day. Plan your big purchases accordingly. Joining organizations such as AAA or American Association of Retired Persons (AARP) can give you preferred pricing in a host of places, too.

RESPONDING TO SOCIETAL PROBLEMS

In this book you've learned about two government programs that were created to help individuals and families. They are, of course:

- Social Security—supports older and disabled Americans who cannot work
- Medicare/Medicaid—provides medical insurance for older or poor Americans

Other initiatives, either private or public, facilitate people giving their time to help those who need it, both in this country and internationally. Among some of the better known are:

- Peace Corps: www.peacecorps.gov
- AmeriCorps: www.nationalservice.gov/programs/americorps
- Habitat for Humanity: www.habitat.org
- Doctors Without Borders: www.doctorswithoutborders.org
- City Year: www.cityyear.org
- Red Cross: www.redcross.org

Service organizations offer individuals like yourself structured opportunities to offer a helping hand to those in need. Through them, you can help alleviate suffering or provide basic human needs like food, shelter, or healthcare.

Giving Back to Get Back

Working closely with people suffering a true need such as hunger can educate the volunteer about the root causes of the problem. The person being helped has as much to give by sharing the experience of her need with the person offering assistance. She is an expert in the topic of her need.

You and your compatriots are more than likely going to be the architects of entirely new ways of responding to social problems, bringing fresh views and an abundance of "can-do" energy to the task of conquering stubborn issues like homelessness and chronic hunger. You are accustomed to breaking the rules, thinking outside the box, doing it your way. You're not going to stop seeking better ways now.

DOWN BUT NOT OUT

Life transitions don't always go perfectly smoothly, even with the best of planning. Sometimes events happen that will force you to make adjustments to the grand plan. You may think you have all your ducks in order to leave your company at your full retirement age with a pretty good nest egg. You may have been disciplined, saving enough funds to enable you to live work-free and go on safari, fund family reunions at a Disney theme park, or chuck it all and sail around the world. This plan might be ditched when, in your late fifties but well before retirement, you experience any of the following sudden events:

- Your company has massive layoffs, you included.
- You become disabled, limiting your mobility drastically.
- You have to assume guardianship for a family member.
- Your 401(k) investments are wiped out.

As devastating as any of these situations would be, you can work your way through them, or any other setback, developing a Plan B. Americans are blessed with a broad streak of optimism. If you suffer a major financial setback in the years encroaching upon retirement, you may panic thinking that you do not have enough years left to recoup what you have lost. The financial loss may mean you have to abandon plans for your gilded retirement life. It might further mean you have to defer your departure from the ranks of the rank and file for a few more years. Depending on other resources available to you, including Social Security and other savings, you may be able to proceed with your retirement timeline, but find you will be swimming at the community pool and not at the beaches of Antigua. Look at the bright side—at least you will not be tied to a job.

Forced Into Taking Early Benefits

Throughout this book, we've recommended against taking early Social Security benefits when you turn sixty-two. Still, that's when a majority of beneficiaries start taking them. Often the reason is a layoff. If this happens to you, taking early benefits may be your only option. But it's not one to rush into, since it will permanently fix your monthly benefit at a lower level. Carefully consider all other options before taking this step and see if it's at all possible to hold on financially until you reach your full retirement age.

BOUNCING BACK

Most setbacks are not insurmountable. They definitely change the picture, challenging you to come up with coping strategies. When you suffer a financial blow, your basic choices boil down to spending less, saving more, or both.

Spending less may seem unappealing at first blush because you feel you are being deprived of a life you thought you had all figured out. But by using a little creativity you should be able to construct a joyful, enriching, and full life. Just because you cannot have a Rolex doesn't mean you cannot have a watch.

INDEX

Annuities, investing in, 211
Appealing SSA decisions, 148–52
Applying for Social Security. *See also*
    Disability benefits
    documents needed, 59
    how to apply, 55–56
    information needed for, 56–58
    online, 55
    in person, 56
    on the phone, 56
Australia, social security in, 121
Average indexed monthly earnings
    (AIME), 50, 51, 131–33, 134

Baby names lists, 10
Benefits. *See also* Eligibility for
    Social Security; Spousal benefits;
    Suspending benefits
    adjusting, as option to fix system,
        32–33
    annual earnings limit, 108–10
    applying for. *See* Applying for Social
        Security
    average indexed monthly earnings
        (AIME), 50, 51, 131–33, 134
    break-even analysis for late benefits,
        117–20
    claiming later, 111, 113, 117–21,
        188–90
    cost-of-living adjustment (COLA)
        adjustments, 19, 29, 32, 134
    deemed filing and, 126–30
    deposit options, 60
    early, 111–16, 234
    estimating, Social Security
        statement and, 60–64
    factors affecting amount, 49–51
    increasing, with delayed credits,
        57–58
    life expectancy and, 114–15, 116, 117,
        118, 188

payment of, 60, 147
pensions and, 91, 137–39
reduced, 29–30
retroactive, 58
retroactive lump sum option, 140–43
stopping, 144–47
taxes on, 102–5
tracking, 187–88
Windfall Elimination Provision,
    131–36
Bismarck, Otto von, 14, 18, 142
Bonds, investing in, 210–11
Budgets, 185, 225–26. *See also*
    Financial and retirement planning;
    Savings
Business, starting, 221

Canada, OAS pensions in, 22
Card, Social Security. *See* Social
    Security number/card
Carter, Jimmy, 222–23
Children
    benefits for, 97–101
    child-in-care, 98, 99–100
    with disabilities, 77–81
    of divorced parents, 101
    of retired parents, 98
Cost-of-living adjustment (COLA)
    adjustments, 19, 29, 32, 134

Death
    illness before, 88
    lump-sum benefit, 89
    survivors benefits, 87–91
Deemed filing, 126–30
Defined-benefit plans, 199
Defined-contribution plans, 200–206
    choosing right investments for,
        210–11
    Employee Stock Ownership Plans
        (ESOPs), 200–201, 211

Defined-contribution plans—*continued*
    401(k) plans, 107, 186, 200, 201–5, 207
    403(b) plans, 200, 205–6, 207
    457 plans, 200, 206
    thrift or savings plans (TSAs), 201
Disability benefits, 65–71
    about: overview of, 65
    annual payment total, 11
    appealing decisions, 69–70, 148–52
    applying for, 67–70, 76, 78–79
    benefit calculation (SSI), 74–76
    children with disabilities, 77–81
    earnings tests, 66–67
    eligibility for, 66–67, 68–69, 73–74,
        77–80
    family/dependent benefits, 69, 70
    other benefits and, 70
    Qualified Disabled and Working
        Individuals Program (QDWI),
        170–71
    SNAP and, 73, 76
    SSDI (Social Security Disability
        Insurance), 65–70
    SSI (Supplemental Security Income),
        72–76
    Ticket to Work and, 70–71
Divorce. *See also* Remarriage
    benefit eligibility and, 48, 82, 87, 89
    changing Social Security card name
        and, 40
    child-in-care and, 99–100
    children of divorced parents, 101
    deemed filing and, 127

Early benefits, 111–16, 234
Earning money, Social Security and.
    See Working in retirement
Eligibility for Social Security. *See also*
    Benefits
    aging population size and, 19
    expanding coverage and, 31–32
    expansion of, 19
    first/early beneficiaries, 16
    raising full retirement age and, 32–33
    who doesn't qualify, 50
    who qualifies, 11, 47–49

Employee Stock Ownership Plans
    (ESOPs), 200–201, 211

FICA (Federal Insurance Contributions
    Act) tax, 8, 26, 47, 72, 102
File and suspend, 10, 83, 128–29, 142
Financial and retirement planning. *See
    also* Benefits; Defined-contribution
    plans; Individual retirement
    accounts (IRAs); Savings
    asking Social Security questions, 193
    career challenges and, 219
    choosing right investments, 210–11
    financial planners/life coaches for,
        192–96, 229–30
    flexibility in, 219–21
    helpful habits/tips, 185–87
    importance of, 184, 185
    life planning, 225, 226–31
    overcoming challenges, 219, 233–34
    planning for income, 225
    Social Security future and, 212
    spending habits and, 186–87
    spouse/partner and, 230–31
    when to start, 197–99
Fixing Social Security, 30–33
Food stamps. *See* SNAP
Foreign countries
    immigrants/visa-holders from, 51
    living/working in, Social Security
        benefits and, 94–96
    Medicare in, 162
    social insurance in, 21, 22, 121, 127,
        142, 145, 187, 216
401(k) plans, 107, 186, 200, 201–5, 207
403(b) plans, 200, 205–6, 207
457 plans, 200, 206
FRA. *See* Full retirement age (FRA)
France, social security in, 127
Full retirement age (FRA)
    applying for benefits and, 56–58
    delayed retirement credits and,
        57–58
    determining, 52–54
    raising, as option to fix Social
        Security, 32–33

retroactive benefits and, 58
stopping benefits before/at, 144–47
Funding social security, 24–27
  bankruptcy concerns, 28–30
  cap on contributions, 25, 63
  depletion of funds, 26
  fixing, alternatives, 30–33
  immigrant and visa-holder
    contributions, 51
  percent of income contributed, 25, 63
  Ponzi schemes and, 24–25
  raiding of funds and, 25
  sources of funds, 26
  younger generation and, 26–27

Germany, social security in, 142
Government Pension Offset, 91, 137–39
Great Society, 155, 178

Happiness in retirement, 213–16
Healthcare, Social Security and,
  153–58, 191. *See also* Medicaid;
  Medicare; Prescriptions
Health Insurance Premium Payment
  Program (HIPP), 180
History of Social Security
  Bismarck and, 14, 18, 142
  events leading to Social Security,
    12–14
  expanding beneficiaries, 16
  first beneficiaries, 16
  origins, 12–17
  retirement history and, 18–19
  rise of middle class, retirement class,
    20–23
  Roosevelt and, 13–14, 15, 16
  scope of act creating, 15–16
Hoover, Herbert, and Hoovervilles,
  12–13

Identity theft, Social Security number
  and, 42–46
Individual retirement accounts (IRAs)
  choosing best for you, 209
  choosing right investments for,
    210–11

contribution limits, 206, 207
maximizing 401(k) and 403(b)
  contributions before, 107
Roth, 207, 208, 209
SEP, 201, 208
setting up, 186, 206–7
SIMPLE, 201, 208
traditional, 207, 209
types of, 186, 206
withdrawing money from, 207
Insurance, social, 8–11
Interest-free loan, 130
Investing. *See also* Defined-
  contribution plans; Individual
  retirement accounts (IRAs); Savings
  in annuities, 211
  choosing investments, 210–11
  in ESOPs, 211
  in stocks, bonds, mutual funds,
    210–11

Jail time, benefits and, 11, 68
Johnson, Lyndon, 154, 155. *See also*
  Great Society

Keogh plans, 209–10

Life expectancy, benefits and, 114–15,
  116, 117, 118, 188
Life planning. *See* Financial and
  retirement planning
Loan, interest-free, 130
Low-income workers
  healthcare for. *See* Medicaid
  Low-Income Subsidy (Extra Help),
    154, 168–69
  prescription drug assistance, 167–71
  SLMB for, 170
  Social Security benefitting, 11,
    133–36

Marriage. *See* Remarriage; Spousal
  benefits
Medicaid, 178–83
  about: overview of, 155–56, 178
  coverages, 181

Medicaid—*continued*
    Great Society and, 155, 178
    Health Insurance Premium Payment
        Program (HIPP), 180
    Medicare Savings Programs and,
        169–71
    origins of, 178–79
    qualifying/applying for, 179–81, 183
    resource for information, 181
    spend-down programs, 182–83
Medicare, 159–66. *See also*
    Prescriptions
    abroad, 162
    changing plans, 163
    civil rights and, 154
    coverages, 159–66
    credits to qualify for, 62
    dealing with spending increases,
        157–58
    for disabled children, 81
    eligibility for, 81, 156–58
    enrolling in, 164, 165
    functions of, 155
    Great Society and, 178
    no cap on contributions, 63
    origins of, 154
    Part A, 155, 159–61
    Part B, 155, 161–62
    Part C. *See* Medicare Advantage
    Part D, 155, 164–65, 168
    paying for growth in spending,
        157–58
    penalty for delayed sign-up, 165, 168
    Savings Programs (QDWI, QI, QMB,
        SLMB), 169–71
    tax paid to support, 26, 63, 122–23,
        157–58
    uncovered expenses, 165–66
Medicare Advantage (Medicare Part C)
    about, 55, 163–64
    doctors accepting, 174–75
    enrolling in, 175–76
    Medigap to cover gaps, 156, 176–77
    plan ratings, 172
    private plans, 172–75
    reviewing/comparing plans, 173

Medigap plans, 156, 176–77
Military
    benefits, Social Security and, 93–94
    veteran benefits, 92–93
Minorities, Social Security importance
    for, 135
Mutual funds, investing in, 210–11
my Social Security account, 39, 64,
    187–88, 212

Native Americans, Social Security and,
    90
The New Deal, 13
Noncitizens, Social Security and, 37–38,
    51

Online account (*my* Social Security), 39,
    64, 187–88, 212

PASS (Plan to Achieve Self-Support), 80
Payroll taxes. *See* Taxes, payroll
Pensions
    defined-benefit plans, 199
    Social Security and, 91, 137–39
    vanishing, 199
Perkins, Frances, 14
Planning. *See* Benefits; Financial and
    retirement planning; Savings
Ponzi schemes, 24–25
Prescriptions
    assistance with costs, 167–71
    cost of, 167
    Extra Help, 168–69
    extreme cost example, 167
    Medicare Savings Programs and,
        169–71
    Part D coverage, 155, 164–65, 168
Primary insurance amount (PIA),
    85–86, 134, 142–43, 187–88
Privatizing Social Security, 30
Protecting Social Security number, 42–46

Qualified Disabled and Working
    Individuals Program (QDWI), 170–71
Qualified Medicare Beneficiary
    Program (QMB), 170

Qualifying for Social Security. *See* Eligibility for Social Security
Qualifying Individual Program (QI), 170
Questions, asking about Social Security, 193

Remarriage, 48, 88, 101
Replacing Social Security card, 39–40
Retirement. *See also* Defined-contribution plans; Financial and retirement planning; Individual retirement accounts (IRAs); Savings; Working in retirement
 birth of retired class, 20–23
 boomer generation philosophy, 224
 contributing to society in, 222–23
 delaying benefits/claiming later, 111, 113, 117–21, 188–90
 finding happiness in, 213–16
 forward-thinking approach, 221–23
 healthcare expenses and, 191. *See also* Healthcare, Social Security and; Medicaid; Medicare
 history of, 18–19
 ideal, creating, 217–18
 income sources in, 190–91
 keeping track of Social Security, 187–88
 leisure time, 22
 more than just fun, 23
 overcoming challenges, 219, 233–34
 planning for. *See also* Benefits; Financial and retirement planning; Savings
 responding to societal problems and, 231–32
 Social Security and, 184–91
 spending habits, 186–87
 volunteering in, 227, 232
Retroactive benefits, 58
Retroactive lump sum option, 140–43
Roosevelt, Franklin D., 13–14, 15, 16

Saving Programs, Medicare (QDWI, QI, QMB, SLMB), 169–71

Savings. *See also* Defined-contribution plans; Financial and retirement planning; Individual retirement accounts (IRAs)
 budgets and, 185, 225–26
 choosing right investments, 210–11
 defined-benefit plans, 199
 employer matching, 107, 186, 201–4
 employer-sponsored plans, 186, 199
 frugal lifestyle and, 186–87
 importance of, 185
 investing when young, 198
 Keogh plans, 209–10
 personal plans, 186
SECA (Self-Employment Contributions Act), 8
Self-employment, 122–25
 deductions, 123
 Medicare tax, 157
 retirement savings. *See* Defined-contribution plans; Individual retirement accounts (IRAs); Keogh plans
 SECA and, 8
 taxes and, 25, 122–23, 157
 tax forms, 125
 wages and earnings, 123, 124–25
SEP (simplified employee pension) plans, 201, 208
SHIP (State Health Insurance Assistance Program), 181
SIMPLE (savings incentive match) plans, 201, 208
SNAP (Supplementary Nutritional Assistance Program), 73, 76
Social insurance/security
 how Social Security compares, 145
 in other countries, 21, 22, 121, 127, 142, 145, 187, 216
 Social Security as, 8–11
Social Security
 about: overview of, 5–6, 7–8
 benefitting low-income workers, 11, 133–36
 fact and figures, 9
 funding of, 8

Social Security—*continued*
   my Social Security online account,
      39, 64, 187–88, 212
   in other countries, 21, 22
   payouts annually, 9
   as social insurance, 8–11
   tracking, 187–88
Social Security Administration (SSA)
   contacting, asking questions, 193
   origin/creation of, 15–16
   other programs operated, 10
   trust funds and, 9–10, 11, 25, 26, 28
Social Security number/card
   getting new card, 34–38
   name changes and, 40–41
   noncitizens and, 37–38
   protecting, identity theft and, 42–46
   replacing card, 39–40
Society, responding to problems of,
   231–32
Spain, social security in, 216
Specified Low-Income Medicare
   Beneficiary Program (SLMB), 170
Spend-down programs, 182–83
Spousal benefits, 82–86. *See also*
   Divorce
   child-in-care and, 98
   common-law marriage and, 84–85
   file and suspend and, 83
   marriage definition/same-sex
      marriage and, 48, 84
   online calculator for, 86
   primary insurance amount (PIA),
      85–86, 134, 142–43, 187–88
   retirement planning and, 230–31
   survivors benefits, 87–91
   whether to file, 82–83
SSDI and SSI. *See* Disability benefits
State Health Insurance Assistance
   Program (SHIP), 181
Statement, Social Security, 60–64
Stocks, investing in, 210–11
Stopping benefits, 144–47
Supplemental Security Income (SSI),
   10, 11, 65–67, 72–76
Survivors benefits, 87–91

Suspending benefits
   changes effective January, 2016,
      126–28
   deemed filing and, 126–30
   file and suspend, 10, 83, 128–29, 142
Sweden, social security in, 21

Taxes, on benefits, 102–5
Taxes, payroll
   FICA, 26, 47, 72, 102
   raising, as option to fix system, 31
   SECA, 8
   trust funds and, 9–10, 11, 25, 26, 28
Taxes, self-employment, 25, 122–23,
   125, 157
Ticket to Work, 70–71
Townsend, Dr. Francis, 13–14
Tracking your Social Security, 187–88
Trust funds, 9–10, 11, 25, 26, 28
TSAs (thrift or savings plans), 201

United Kingdom, social security in, 187

Veteran benefits, 92–93
Volunteering, 227, 232

Webb, Dell, 20–21
Winant, John G., 15
Windfall Elimination Provision, 131–36
Working in retirement, 106–10
   age discrimination and, 189
   annual earnings limit, 108–10
   benefits of, 106–8
   delaying benefits and, 111, 113,
      117–21, 188–90
   ideas for delaying benefits as long as
      possible, 188–90
   income sources and, 190–91
   retraining and, 222